"Whether you're a newly minted graduate or a seasoned job seeker, you'll find this book extraordinarily useful. *The Job Seeker's Script* shows you how to communicate the value you will bring to a hiring organization throughout your job search. The ability to put forward your skills, accomplishments, and background in an inspiring way is often the greatest challenge for job seekers, and readers will discover how to create and deliver the right messaging to get hired."

—**Jodyi Wren,** interim assistant dean, executive director, and assistant vice provost for Career Education Initiatives, Gwen M. Greene Center for Career Education and Connections, University of Rochester

"*The Job Seeker's Script* is an impressive, extraordinarily useful book that provides a step-by-step process for selling yourself successfully throughout your job search. Whether you want to move up the ladder in your present company or are seeking a job elsewhere, this book is a must-read."

—**Chris Kowalewski,** chief growth officer, Compass Group

"I can vouch for the brilliance of this book from personal experience. Judith Humphrey has been my communications coach, and she taught me how to script myself for every meeting and every interview. As a result, I've gone into each encounter confidently knowing exactly how to 'tell my story.' This has made all the difference and has enabled me to build a successful career. Readers of the book will find the same success."

—**Adeola Adebayo,** senior managing director, Sustainable Investments, Canada Life

"*The Job Seeker's Script* offers superb advice: tell your story well. As the head of an executive recruiting firm, I ask candidates about their story: what they've learned, why they made the moves they made, how they've accomplished things, why they left certain jobs, and even why they made certain ethical decisions. Judith Humphrey's inspiring book equips readers to script themselves for every encounter with a standout narrative. I highly recommend it to all job candidates."

—**Jay Rosenzweig,** founder and CEO, Rosenzweig & Company, "Building the Leadership Teams of Tomorrow"

"In a crowded field of advice, *The Job Seeker's Script* stands out. When I talk to candidates at all levels, sometimes their pitches don't come across as authentic. This important and well-crafted book explains how to put a genuine pitch together, what the key elements are, and how to make sure it comes from your core, your heart. That gets my attention and keeps these job seekers top of mind."

—**Amanda Luthra,** senior freelance recruiter

"This book is a treasure. The author, Judith Humphrey, coached me on its lessons. As a result, I aced my med school interviews and received a fellowship at the University of Toronto medical school. I'm now an MD and a specialist. Want a successful career? Buy the book!"

—**Robert Mitchell, MD,** Fraser Hospital, British Columbia

THE Job Seeker's SCRIPT

Tell Your Story and
Land Your Dream Position

JUDITH HUMPHREY

FAST
COMPANY
Press

Fast Company Press
New York, New York
www.fastcompanypress.com

This work is being published under the Fast Company Press imprint by an exclusive arrangement with *Fast Company*. *Fast Company* and the *Fast Company* logo are registered trademarks of Mansueto Ventures, LLC. The Fast Company Press logo is a wholly owned trademark of Mansueto Ventures, LLC.

Distributed by Greenleaf Book Group

For ordering information or special discounts for bulk purchases, please contact Greenleaf Book Group at PO Box 91869, Austin, TX 78709, 512.891.6100.

Design and composition by Greenleaf Book Group
Cover design by Greenleaf Book Group
Cover images copyright abzee, 2009;
Used under license from Shutterstock.com

Publisher's Cataloging-in-Publication data is available.

Print ISBN: 978-1-63908-025-0

eBook ISBN: 978-1-63908-026-7

To offset the number of trees consumed in the printing of our books, Greenleaf donates a portion of the proceeds from each printing to the Arbor Day Foundation. Greenleaf Book Group has replaced over 50,000 trees since 2007.

Printed in the United States of America on acid-free paper

23 24 25 26 27 28 29 30   10 9 8 7 6 5 4 3 2 1

First Edition

For every job seeker who has a story to tell

Contents

Introduction

Our hiring is almost completely built around just
going through someone's life story.[1]

—TOBI LÜTKE, CEO, SHOPIFY

TELLING YOUR STORY in a compelling way is the key to landing that coveted job. This book will show you how to create a winning narrative for each stage in your job search.

But first, I'll share my own story and explain why I wrote this book. I founded a company, The Humphrey Group, 35 years ago to teach leaders how to communicate. As a speechwriter for CEOs I could see that many VPs hadn't any idea how to craft their speeches. They weren't exactly getting booed by their audiences. But their speeches and presentations were non-starters. And they realized it.

I thought "Why not create a business to show them how to script themselves?"

So I launched the company.

It was exciting to be an entrepreneur and build a firm that helped executives get their messages across. I loved growing the business, not only in Toronto, but globally. We helped clients create their scripts, their speaking notes, and answers to questions.

I also hired actors who helped our clients—and me—understand the importance of "presence" and a strong delivery. One of our actors was Marshall Bell, who has appeared in many movies, and was filming *Twins* about the time he joined us. The actors coached clients on their delivery: everything from vocal power to stance.

Imagine my excitement—we were launching something that hadn't existed.

Most of our work in the first years was at the executive level—and those contacts proved to be my link to the world of job seekers. I say that because one day, a senior client said, "Do you have a minute?" Of course I did. He continued, "My daughter wants to be a doctor and has several medical school interviews coming up. Can you help her?"

"I would be happy to," I replied.

I met with the daughter, and we made a list of the questions she might be asked. Over several sessions, we scripted what she would say, using the same template I had taught her father and our other clients to use in their speeches and off-the-cuff remarks. I rehearsed her to make sure she delivered her answers clearly, confidently, and naturally. She went to the interviews knowing they would seal her fate and career destiny.

What happened? She nailed the interviews—and was accepted into every medical school she applied to. Those scripting techniques that we'd been teaching to our executive clients made all the difference to her. She is now a practicing physician in a major hospital. She was the first of many job candidates I coached using the scripting techniques featured in this book. In the months and years that followed, I prepared other young people and many senior clients for job interviews. Our success rate was 100 percent! I was thrilled that this coaching led to amazing careers for job seekers.

My own career had in fact been built on the power of the script. Even before I launched my company, scripting was my superpower. I not only used it in my jobs as a speech ("script") writer. I used it to *get* those jobs, scripting myself for each job interview, and rehearsing those narratives so I'd deliver the best story about myself.

My desire to write this book emerges from this long-time belief in the power of a persuasive script. These personal successes and my continuing work with job seekers enable me to say that you, too, will benefit from creating a great narrative when looking for your next job. Scripting yourself can be your superpower!

These turbulent, challenging times in the job market demand a book like this. More than ever, job seekers are leaving their current positions either for greener pastures elsewhere or to advance within their company. This is the era of the "Great Resignation," also known as the "Great Reshuffle." There are now more individuals competing for positions. At the same time, companies have become more demanding. Firms are eager to hire and retain employees, even with the ups and downs of the economy. But they want only the best talent—individuals with daring and determination who will immediately add value to the company and, ideally, stay with them.

The bar has been set high, and job seekers need to be at their very best to land their desired position, whether they're seeking to rise within an organization or move to another company. This book will give you a new set of skills that will set you apart. The ability to present your narrative clearly and forcefully will serve you well in your job search and throughout your career.

The Need for This Book

Today's job seeker confronts an endless stream of advice. Career counselors, friends, advisors, and authors tell candidates to polish their elevator pitch, network with everyone under the sun, improve their social media presence, write their resume carefully, appeal to the robot, proofread everything they write, draft a personal cover letter, rehearse for tough interviews, and prepare for any question that might be thrown their way. All of this is great advice. But candidates still struggle with the job search process; it can be a long and winding road. Even in a job seeker's market, there may be hundreds of candidates for each position. And there are so many things to think about if you want to be job worthy.

But there is one all-important area that has not been covered enough—knowing how to tell your story throughout your job journey. This involves creating and delivering a series of strong, compelling scripts. To do this requires the communication skills and mastery of persuasion discussed in this book.

To stand out, you must create an inspiring script at each step of the job journey. Inspire in your brief elevator pitch, your informal chats, your networking conversations, your resume and cover letter, your spot-on responses in interviews, and the thoughtful and genuine way you follow up to thank the people with whom you've had meaningful interactions. *The Job Seeker's Script* will show you how to script yourself for success at every turn and with everyone you meet.

It doesn't matter whether you are "speaking" in person or on paper. All these scripts represent a continuous narrative designed to tell your story and persuade others that you are the ideal candidate for a job. The individual scripts provide a format for telling a clear, linear, and concise story to those you're with.

Scripting yourself convincingly is the secret to getting hired because if someone believes in you, they will help you get that job. They'll be keen to be part of your network and recommend you. They'll feel excitement when they read your resume and cover letter. They'll actively advocate on your behalf. And they'll connect with you during the interview. Your success in the job market will depend upon your ability to turn others into believers at every stage in the process with your brilliant words and standout story.

You won't *sound* scripted. Job seekers want to be—and need to be—relaxed and in the moment. This book is not about memorizing your scripts verbatim. It is about preparing, knowing what you're going to say, and going into those situations with the confidence that comes from planning your words and messages while delivering them with apparent spontaneity and everyday language. You will learn to do all this and more. In short, you'll discover a new voice and a narrative that will equip you to ace every conversation and every written document you submit.

Telling Your Story

Your entire job journey involves telling a compelling story. Building this narrative is a highly creative process that includes preparing what you'll say, internalizing your material, rehearsing your lines, and delivering your words in an authentic and captivating way—throughout the job journey. This book will take you through the entire scripting process, showing you how to craft genuine, persuasive, and consistent scripts that inspire your networking contacts, recruiters, hiring managers, and future bosses.

In a typical job search, you'll need many stellar scripts: an elevator pitch, a networking script, a resume script, a cover letter script, a rehearsal script, and various interview scripts. All of these, if well designed, will contribute to a cohesive whole. They will enable you to deliver a clear, compelling, and persuasive message about yourself as a job candidate. You'll describe yourself at each turn in a way that will make others see you as an exceptional candidate.

This book will give you a scripting template for organizing what you say (and what you write). The template has four structural components, which together spell HIRE:

Hook—reach out to your audience with a grabber
Inspire—articulate your message
Reinforce—develop your message
Engage—state your call to action

This template, illustrated throughout the book, is scalable. It can be used for a 30-second elevator pitch or for a full interview. The HIRE template will enable you to structure your conversations and written communications and get a strong, clear, and passionately felt message across throughout your job search.

This book will also introduce you to the best language to use for your scripts. You will discover words that show a positive, confident, and enthusiastic outlook. You don't want to come across as someone who is overselling yourself, but you don't want to undersell yourself either. You want to be humble, but you don't want that to look like you lack confidence. You want to be passionate, but you don't want to overdo the zeal in cheerleader fashion. You want to move others with your words when they hear you speak or write. Every chapter will discuss the language to use for various scripts.

Finally, this book will show how to rehearse your remarks and deliver a standout performance. When you rehearse your lines, you'll want to own the script—then internalize it. When you walk into the room for a networking meeting or a job interview, you won't hem and haw or say, "Uh, let me think about that" or "I'm not sure."

You'll learn from this book how to be on top of what you want to say and deliver with confidence. You'll stand out whether the meeting is in person or on Zoom. You'll achieve a strong presence, know how to listen well, ask the best questions, and stay on script in a way that shows confidence and clear messaging. You'll learn all these things—and much more.

How to Use This Book

This book is divided into four parts, and all four parts will play a role in your success.

"Part I: You Are the Scriptwriter: Telling Your Story" will guide you through all the elements that make for a well-structured and well-delivered narrative. You'll learn how to define your goals, develop a story line that leads to that next job, and project your best qualities as the main character in your successful career journey. You'll discover how to formulate your overarching message for the story you'll be telling about yourself. And you'll learn to use a clear four-step process for organizing each script, so it is powerfully persuasive. Finally, you will discover the importance of internalizing these scripts as you prepare for each conversation and interview.

In short, Part I of this book gives you all the tools you'll need to script yourself for success in your job journey. Parts II, III, and IV show how to create your scripts as you move through the various stages of your job search.

"Part II: Conversational Scripts" discusses how to develop the informal scripts that form the essence of what you'll say in the early stages of your job search. This section focuses on the pitches you'll make in short encounters (the elevator pitch), emails, phone calls, networking meetings, and conversations about a promotion within your present company. These scripts may feel casual, but they deserve the same preparation as the more serious scripts require. Well scripted, you will be off to a great start.

"Part III: Written Scripts" will show you how to tell your story during the middle stage of your job journey, when you'll need to prepare resumes, cover letters, and thank-you notes. These may seem like documents with prescribed formats, but they need to be crafted with your story line in mind. You want to keep the focus on developing a clear and consistent narrative.

"Part IV: Interview Scripts" will show you how to tell your story in the final stages of your job search. It will guide you in preparing for those crucial interviews and mastering interview techniques. This phase of your journey begins with intensive research on the company, its culture, the people who will interview you, and the job itself.

You will also learn how to craft your interview pitch, prepare for Q&A, get ready for off-the-wall quirky questions, imagine what you'd say if you were interviewed by a CEO, and deliver a great performance during every interview you have. You'll even discover what to say in a follow-up letter if you don't hear from the hiring company and you want to keep the opportunity alive. With all this preparation—and an understanding of what it takes to deliver a standout performance—you'll be sure to win that coveted job.

The chapters in this book will take you through your entire job search journey and show you the power of scripting yourself successfully at each turn. Nobody will ask to see your script, and nobody will even know that you've prepared and learned one for that occasion. But they will feel the power of it. The scripting techniques featured in this book will enable you to sell yourself successfully and get hired.

Let's dive in and start by deciding what your story line will be. It will shape your entire journey and every script you deliver along the way.

PART I

YOU ARE THE SCRIPTWRITER: TELLING YOUR STORY

Whether you're on the job market for the first time and looking to launch your career, or you are a seasoned professional, telling your story is essential for landing the job you want. But how do you do this? The chapters in Part I will show you how to create your story line, define your character, create a guiding message, structure each conversation, and rehearse for every encounter.

CHAPTER 1

Deciding on Your Story Line

"Would you tell me, please, which way I ought
to go from here?"

"That depends a good deal on where you want
to get to," said the Cat.

"I don't much care where—" said Alice.

"Then it doesn't much matter
which way you go," said the Cat.[1]

THESE LINES FROM LEWIS CARROLL'S *Alice's Adventures in Wonderland* provide guidance to today's job seekers: if you want to land that next job, you must know where you're going. Creating your narrative involves knowing what you're seeking in a job and what kind of company you are looking for. Think of yourself as a scriptwriter, creating a plot or story line by deciding where you want to go. Doing so will not only help you with your next move but with your entire career.

Do you want to stay with your present employer? If so, consider a more senior role in your department or another area of the company. Or perhaps you want a role that's at the same level but in a totally different space. If you like the company you're with and you see opportunities that you'd like to pursue, go for it. Companies are facing a talent crunch, and they would love to keep and promote their best employees. As other people move on, there will be an increasing number of internal positions available.

Talk to your boss, a mentor, or a sponsor about what opportunities might await you in your present firm. If you have had a successful career trajectory at your current firm, it's likely you will continue to flourish there. All the techniques you'll learn from this book will enable you to communicate like a pro and win those big jobs in your present company.

If you decide you want a different environment or a different culture altogether, look toward the exit door. Hundreds of thousands of jobs are posted every month. Invitations turn up on your LinkedIn site. Recruiters offer still more possibilities. Job fairs might entice you. Friends make suggestions.

Many of these advertised jobs, however, will not be a good fit for you.

If your background doesn't dovetail with the listing, you'll waste your time and the recruiter's in applying. And even when you do get a job offer, you should ask yourself: Is the position a wise choice? Is the job the next step or a detour in my journey? Will I be happy if I go to that company, and where will it lead? With so many options, there's a need to manage your career choices so that one job builds on another, and they collectively point in the direction you want to go. But what is that direction?

This first chapter shows you how to set yourself on the right footing by gaining the self-knowledge that guides your job search.

The Six Questions to Ask Yourself

People are leaving their current jobs in greater numbers than in previous decades. A survey by the firms Accounting Principals and Ajilon found that over 80 percent of full-time workers are actively seeking or open to new job opportunities.[2] There are many possibilities and many decisions to make. Here are the six essential questions to ask yourself to help decide the direction you wish to pursue.

#1 AM I PREPARED TO INVEST IN MYSELF?

Before you begin, decide whether you're willing to invest the time and effort a successful job search requires. This is an important question. In fact, it's the most important one because for you to land your dream job, you'll need to put in considerable time and thought. Not everyone is willing to carve out that time, especially if they're already working. According to a 2022 report, more than 70 percent of job candidates will not submit a job application if it takes more than 15 minutes to complete.[3] That's a formula for failure if you're taking the job hunt seriously. If you really want a new job, invest the time and don't get discouraged. Stay on the path that will lead to success.

#2 WHAT ARE MY SKILLS AND INTERESTS?

It's time to assess what you're good at and what really interests you. If you're honestly assessing your skills, what are they? And what turns you on? "Know thyself" is all-important when thinking about how you can excel.

Are you a specialist or a leader? Sure, you can be both, but most people put themselves on one side or the other of this divide. A specialist might be an art director or copywriter in an advertising agency, or a speechwriter, or perhaps an accountant or engineer. People in these positions don't work in total isolation, but they are often happiest sitting at a desk tackling a project by themselves.

The leader, on the other hand, wants to be out there inspiring a team and coordinating larger undertakings. A leader at any level likely has people skills or other "soft skills" like the willingness to listen, empathize, and collaborate. In short, a leader has the qualities that inspire others. Ask yourself which type of person you are and whether you want to continue playing that same role.

Be realistic in what you can honestly say are your skill strengths. If you have your eye on a job category, but you're missing a necessary skill, take some training.

Follow the advice of Joseph Testani, deputy to the president at the University of Rochester and former head of the university's career center. He advises: "If you see a gap in your experience that's related to a job you're interested in, build a skill on a platform such as LinkedIn and network with people in that area to mitigate any shortcomings. For example, if a job calls for data visualization or Salesforce or data analysis—take a class to get a credential stating that you have learned something about that subject. You don't always have to be an expert; an understanding of the topic, how it relates to the business, and showing an ability to learn will go a long way."[4]

If you are fortunate enough to work for a company that makes skills development available to you, all the better! Enroll in these programs and note that in your resume.

#3 DO I WANT A NEW DIRECTION?

Next, decide whether you want to continue in the area of your current employment and training or venture into a new direction. You might be skilled in computer languages or petroleum engineering, for example. You've invested a great deal of your education or your career in that area, so naturally, you should consider continuing in that specialization. Cherish your strengths. But don't let the past lock you in if that path no longer excites you. You may want to break out of that mold. This step can take time to figure out—so don't rush your decision. Preparing for your dream job is hard work. Don't give up. Keep going!

When I was a speechwriter early in my career, I loved the work of supporting CEOs and their direct reports, and I was great at it. So I kept pursuing this one role and selling myself into it. But after about 10 years, I began to feel I'd hit a wall. After several years of thinking about my next step, I decided to become an entrepreneur. It worked out, and the company is still alive and successful after 35 years.

Think carefully about whether you want a new direction, and know when to pivot from your finely tuned skills into another role that builds upon these strengths. One of the key factors in determining when to pivot is whether you are still thriving in the role. Since so many of your waking hours are spent at work, you want to find a position that excites you. Sometimes that means changing jobs and changing again until you find the right fit.

My daughter-in-law, Fang Yu, a millennial job seeker, recently told me she had just accepted a job offer, and it would be her eighth position in 11 years. I asked her, "What prompted your quest?"

She replied, "I've taken every opportunity to get closer to the thing I love. It's been an iterative process. A lot of soul-searching. Finding out exactly what I wanted to do with my career came first, and moving up the ladder came second."

Ask yourself if you're truly inspired by your work. A good way to know if you're ready for something new is to take the alarm clock test, says Rob Barnett, author of *Next Job Best Job: 11 Strategies to Get Hired Now.* "When your alarm goes off and you're in that moment between sleep and waking, are you raring to go or saying 'ugh'?" he asks. "It's a soul speaking moment. If you're saying 'ugh,' then your job is not giving what you need."[5]

#4 WHAT KIND OF CULTURE DO I WANT TO WORK IN?

Today, culture is a huge consideration for any job seeker. There was a time, perhaps in your parents' or grandparents' day, when people simply took a job that promised stability and decent pay. Times have changed. Long-term security, steady raises, and company pensions are in short supply. In our uncertain world, culture has grown more important for job seekers.

In a study by Glassdoor, over three-quarters of employees (77 percent) say they would consider a company's culture before applying there. And almost two-thirds (65 percent) of employees say culture is one of the main reasons they stay in their current job.[6] Another study found culture is the single best predictor of employee satisfaction, ahead of compensation and work-life balance.[7] And not surprisingly, 81 percent of the "World's Most Attractive Employers" say diversity and inclusion is a "very important" part of their recruitment policy.[8]

Organizational psychologist Adam Grant agrees that culture is of supreme importance. He advises: "Before taking a job offer, it's worth asking: Do I want to become more like the people here? You can aspire to change the culture of a group, but don't overlook how the culture will change you."[9]

Here are concerns to explore when evaluating a company's culture.

What is the corporate leadership like? Workers today have high expectations of their leaders. Executives and managers need to be transparent, humble, authentic, fully present, and open to their employees. Today's employees are willing to leave their jobs in search of leaders they admire.

A 2021 study published in the *MIT Sloan Management Review* titled "10 Things Your Corporate Culture Needs to Get Right" found that the top three things employees look for in their culture pertain to their leaders.[10] Of greatest importance is that employees feel respected. Second is that they have supportive leaders. And third is that leaders "live core values." I coached a middle-aged woman in preparation for her job interview and she was strong, confident, and successful in landing the job she wanted. But once she came aboard, she was shocked that her boss repeatedly told her, "Don't talk so much." After a few reprimands like this, she left the company and is looking for a different kind of leadership.

Is the atmosphere hard driving or relaxed? No one style fits every employee, and you want to find your ideal match. My first job was in a fast-paced, high-tech firm where the approach was aggressive and ruthless. After two years, I couldn't take it anymore. I left and went to a bank, where the culture was kinder and gentler. Today, with the burnout rate at historic highs, many individuals won't tolerate an aggressive culture.

Does the company actively address biases in sexism, racism, and other forms of discrimination? Not every firm does. I was once interviewed by the CEO of a major oil company; I had been recommended to him by another CEO. He seemed keen to hire me as his speechwriter. I liked him, thought I could work well with him, and had studied his speeches and liked his thinking. I was about to seal the deal when he remarked: "Well, I assume you won't be having any more children." With that one sentence, he lost me. At 38 years old, I deeply wanted to have a second child and did, in fact, give birth at the age of 44. I decided I didn't want to work for a CEO who wanted confirmation that I wouldn't be adding to my family (and who would so blatantly pose a question that just skirted legality). I passed on the job offer.

Look for companies that include equal opportunity statements in their job postings. These announcements might read: "Our company is an equal opportunity employer that is committed to diversity and inclusion in the workplace. We prohibit discrimination and harassment of any kind based on race, color, sex, religion, sexual orientation, national origin, disability, genetic information, pregnancy, or any other protected characteristic." Such statements provide insight into the company's commitment to addressing bias.

Do the company's values fit with yours? Many employees understandably are concerned with their industry's environmental impact or with corporate policies that affect disadvantaged communities. Make sure any firm you choose fits with the values you hold important.

Does the company allow working from home or demand everyone turn up in the office? Many employees are heading for the exit door because they prefer working from home, and their current employer does not make that possible. When Apple's CEO Tim Cook insisted that everyone return to the office in April 2022 when the COVID-19 pandemic was on the wane, there were protests.[11] A group of employees wrote an open letter to executives criticizing the company's hybrid work pilot program, saying it was inflexible. A 2021 study found that 90 percent of millennials and Gen Zers do not want to return to full-time office work.[12] If you are in that category, you'll want a company with flexible work policies. Or you might want to pursue freelancing. Look for a career that provides your desired balance.

#5 WHAT SIZE COMPANY DO I WANT TO WORK IN?

Like Goldilocks, you want to find a company that's not too large, not too small, but just right—for *you*. What does that ideal company look like?

Do you envision a large, multinational company that has a strong, recognized brand and is most likely a place where you can stay and build your career over time? Or do you prefer a mid-sized firm that has a different vibe? Perhaps you favor a start-up where you can be part of something that's new, exciting, and run by a small team. Small companies can bring an element of excitement; they allow you to work closely with decision-makers. But they might offer less stability and less prospect for advancement (unless it's a rapidly growing company). Getting in on the ground floor of a start-up can be a remarkable opportunity, or it could turn into a foolish gamble if the start-up fails. Think about whether long-term stability or short-term excitement and risk is best for you.

#6 WILL I BE ABLE TO SUCCEED THERE?

Finally, ask yourself whether this company would be a place where you can be successful. Find out what kind of opportunities there are for advancement and whether your career ambitions will be supported by the company. As an indication of just how much they value their employees, find out what salaries are like for different positions and whether they meet with your expectations. Ask about the tenure of employees: Has there been a lot of turnover or do employees tend to stick around? Look at the career trajectory of the leadership team and find out whether they've been promoted within the company.

All these questions should be asked—and answered—before you focus your job search. They will define your goals for your career trajectory, which you want to be an upward one. As Chris Kowalewski, chief growth officer of Compass Group, explained to me: "It's important to go into a company from a position of strength. Ask yourself, 'Is this the right company for me? Will I flourish there?' Come in with your eyes wide open."[13]

Let Those Well-Defined Goals Shape Your Job Search

Once you've addressed these six questions, you'll have a well-defined set of goals. Those goals will shape your job search. They'll help you select the companies you'd like to work for and the job postings you'll respond to.

After you've defined your goals, you'll need to craft a mission statement for your career. This is a statement you make *to yourself* to describe your goals. It will guide you in your search and be the first cut at the message you'll deliver to others in your job search.

Here are a few examples (they vary as widely as the world of job seekers does).

- I'm an experienced HR professional who wants a highly responsible position in a large firm—with the appropriate remuneration.

- I'm a recent liberal arts graduate with strong communication and analytical skills and am open to a broad range of possibilities in a firm that has demonstrated respect for diverse employees.

- I'm a petroleum engineer, fluent in three languages, willing to travel, and looking for a position that is exciting and challenging.

- I'm a highly skilled IT specialist, extraordinarily productive and dependable, and looking for a position in a firm that has a track record of supporting individuals with disabilities.

- My heart and future are with the insurance company I work for—they've invested in me and promoted me, I've turned in a strong performance, and I look forward to continuing doing so in a more elevated role.

These mission statements provide a guide as you move forward and a filter as you look at companies. Your mission statement will help you manage your career and decide which positions to pursue and which ones to pass on. They will focus your search. Instead of applying for 150 jobs, you will focus on the ones that align with your mission statement.

But first, let's talk about the "you" who should be fully present in these statements—the central character of your story.

CHAPTER 2

Developing Your Character

YOU ARE THE MAIN CHARACTER in this story. As the scriptwriter, you need to portray yourself so others connect with you and see you as a deserving candidate. Begin by asking yourself: What qualities do I want to project? What makes me special? And what will make me stand out in the industry or company I am applying to?

If you're going to land that job, you'll want to bring forward your best qualities—those that will allow you to shine in every conversation, every interview, every resume and cover letter, and every job you want to win.

That's a tall order!

And it's challenging because nobody is going to tell you what qualities they're looking for. These won't be listed in the job profile. As *Forbes* columnist Liz Ryan writes: "If you read job ads, you'd think that employers are strictly looking for people with very specific types of experience." But "once you get to a job interview," Ryan explains, "the whole picture changes. Employers are looking for qualities in their new hires that are never listed in the job ad."[1] It's up to you as the scriptwriter to know how to portray yourself as a deserving candidate. This chapter presents nine qualities that will allow you to script yourself for success.

#1 Authenticity

Being authentic is one of the highest-ranked qualities. Just listen to Miranda Kalinowski, top recruiter for Facebook, who says: "Standing out from the 'crowd of applicants' can be done by how you demonstrate your authentic self, your voice and opinion."[2] Similarly, Akhil Saxena, vice president of Amazon's Customer Fulfilment Operations in India, said in a LinkedIn News interview that his best advice for job applicants is to "be your authentic self. Be willing to roll up your sleeves. This is your opportunity, your time, your voice."[3]

You won't get far with any recruiter or hiring manager if you're stiff or unnatural or if you lay out every credential you can think of because you want to look impressive. Kalinowski says, "some candidates send resumes with a long list of capabilities on top, and I think, 'you have to be a superhero to have them all.' Highlight just your greatest strengths—that's more convincing and credible."[4] Authenticity, then, means showing what makes you unique, what is special about you, and what drives you. It doesn't mean parroting the job description. On the contrary, it means believing in yourself and showing your genuine qualities that will serve you well in that desired position.

#2 Positivity

Success comes to those with a positive attitude. Throughout your job journey, write and speak enthusiastically about your career aspirations and the company you are interviewing with. This requires research—plenty of it—so that your enthusiasm is backed by a deep knowledge of that firm and the role you'd like to play. If you're seeking an internal promotion, wow your employer with your commitment to building your career with them and contributing to their success.

Talk, too, about the great opportunities you've had, teachers who inspired you, bosses who have set a high standard, colleagues you worked well with, employees you brought along, and projects you had an opportunity to work on. Praise the companies you've worked for and the mentors you've had. Even if you were fired or let go because of downsizing, mention the benefits of this time off—you took a course, had a side gig, or took care of family members.

Use language that shows your upbeat attitude. Mark Unak, chief technology officer of Forj and formerly CTO of Harqen, a software firm that analyzes job candidates' video interviews, told me that companies look for upbeat language in job candidates. Harqen analyzes candidates using a "positivity index" that evaluates them on a scale from +5 to -5.

At the top of this scale of positivity are superlative words like *absolutely, astonishing, super*, and *love*, as well as collegial words like *relationships* and *team*. Use these high-voltage expressions that show you are a positive person.

At the lower end of the positivity scale are negative words like *abhor, abandon, abusive,* and *terrible*.[5] Employers are looking for positive people, so show your enthusiasm with positive expressions while avoiding negative ones. Never diss your last boss. Never show discouragement about your job search or mention that you've been turned down by 30 companies, most of whom ghosted you. Never go on social media and tell the world that you've become tired of the whole interview process (prospective employers find out about this more than you might think). No one wants to hire a complainer.

#3 Passion

Successful job seekers exude passion. We're drawn to people who give us energy—people who are upbeat and enthusiastic. To show your enthusiasm, talk about your passion to build your career, to contribute to the world, to excel in the job you're applying for and the opportunity it provides. Show your enthusiasm for the company that's interviewing you. In your written communications, use words that convey passion and deep interest. Use expressions like "I am keen to make a contribution," "I have always been interested in," "I loved what I heard," "the team interviewing me would be fun to work with," "I would like to add value and promote engagement," and "I will eagerly await next steps."

One young job seeker I know wrote to her hiring company before her final interview. Here's in part what she said (note the passion in her language): "I admire your corporate culture. It fits well with my mission, which is to use the skill sets I have acquired over the years and apply them to a role that I have passion and heart for. Your firm stands out to me as a company that puts their employees' well-being at the forefront of their business, which is exactly where I want to focus my efforts going forward." She got the job.

If you're being considered for an internal position, pull out all the stops. Tell your boss or the hiring manager how much you like working for the company, how much you appreciate the opportunity you've been given to grow within the company, and how you have benefitted from the networking groups and training the firm provided. Showing passion for your present employer will go a long way to getting you to the next level.

#4 Confidence

Confidence is a must-have quality. If you express confidence in your language and speaking style, you will impress those you're meeting with.

In telling your story, use active verbs that show you *created, built, achieved, led, accomplished*, or *implemented*. For example, if you are asked about your present job or are writing about it in your resume, you might say "I *led* a team through a reorganization and *created* an even stronger, more agile group of high achievers." Avoid nouns when you can use an active verb. Saying "I was a manager" is weaker than saying "I *managed*." Saying "I am an IT specialist" is weaker than saying, "As an IT specialist, I *built* a team that *delivered* results for our global clients." Don't talk about the role you were given; talk about what you accomplished in that role.

Avoid passive verbs; they suggest other people acted in some way and you were the recipient of that action. These include expressions like "I *was led* by," "I *was seen* as," "I *was told*," or "I *was passed over*." Even "I *was promoted*" is less strong than "I *moved ahead* into a new role."

Mark Unak, CTO of the technology firm Forj, notes that the Applicant Tracking System (ATS) can detect confident language. It looks for action verbs that show the candidate has accomplished things and isn't afraid to talk about them—and it gives demerit points for passive verbs. To impress both the human and AI evaluator, use action verbs.[6]

Also, avoid weak verbs like "I think," "I hope," "I want," "I suppose," "I suspect," and "I guess." These expressions tend to create a feeling that you are not sure of what you are saying. They make the speaker sound weak.

In the same vein, avoid hedging words and caveats. Hedging words include "sort of," "kind of," "maybe," and "possibly." Caveats undercut you, and include: "I could be wrong," "I'm not sure," "It's only a thought," or "I didn't express that well."

Candidates who use clear, natural language and avoid jargon in their resumes and interviews convey confidence. It's tempting to use meaningless terminology to hide a lack of understanding or convoluted prose to hit every key word. But it doesn't work—big empty words and contorted sentences don't impress. They show you are not grounded.

Confidence is also reflected in your willingness to be forthcoming about what you want in your next assignment, what you'd like to learn, why you are interested in a specific company or job, and why you feel ready for it. Don't back away from answering questions, even tough ones, with clear, thoughtful responses. And be ready to ask the interviewer questions. You will be respected for sharing your views when you ask these probing questions. All of this will show you feel worthy to take on that next-level role.

#5 Impact

Even more important than the jobs you've had or the courses you've taken is the impact you've had. Closely related to this quality is the ability to solve problems.

Facebook's vice president for global recruiting, Miranda Kalinowski, emphasizes the importance of showing your impact. In an interview with CBS News, she advises, "Shining a light on when in the past you have built something, improved something or shown teamwork, how you have collaborated to create something better than you would have on your own, or why you're passionate about [your company's] mission . . . . These are all effective ways to stand out from the crowd."[7]

Similarly, Google's global head of recruiting, Brendan Castle, stated in a CNBC interview: "The No. 1 thing you want to be thinking about is to tell your story—not just your work experience, but also what you've learned and the accomplishments you're most proud of."[8] Castle offers a few guiding questions—your answers will show your impact:

1. What was your role on each team or in each work situation?
2. How did you contribute to the team?
3. What was the biggest impact you had there?

For example, if someone is applying for an account management role, Castle suggests they write: "Grew revenue from 15 small business clients by 10 percent quarter over quarter by mapping new software features as solutions to their business goals."

Showing quantifiable impact is important, whatever your background. Even if you are fresh out of university, you can talk about the impact you had on a research project or a mentoring role. C-level executives should be able to quantify their impact by focusing on the transformation of their organization during their tenure. Making clear what you've accomplished tells the people you meet along your job journey the impact you're likely to have in the role you're seeking.

#6 Resilience

Today more than ever, job candidates need to show they can rebound from challenging circumstances and help others do so too.

Resilience has become a cornerstone of success in today's business world. We've seen that everything can change before our eyes. People we worked beside are now working from anywhere; jobs that existed before no longer do; new roles and responsibilities have risen in importance. Candidates should show they can deal with the increasing pace of change.

You should be willing to talk about situations when you had a problem, when things didn't turn out as you had hoped or planned, or when you had resistance to your ideas. All these are real-life situations, and your goal in describing them is to take your interviewer behind the scenes and show how you were resilient enough to address problems and work through challenging situations. Hiring managers want to hear these stories. That's why the Q&A often includes such challenges as "Tell me a time when things didn't work out as you expected."

#7 Humility

When telling your story, emphasize your accomplishments—but don't boast. Humility may seem old-school, yet it is a quality worth cultivating. It draws people to you. The word *humility* derives from the Latin word *humus*, meaning "earth;" it literally means being grounded. It means being so sure of yourself that you don't have to call undue attention to yourself. Humility need not be viewed as a weakness or a sign of insecurity. Quite the opposite. The right kind of humility impresses.

Humility is especially important in today's business world because organizations are flatter than ever, and acting superior doesn't cut it. Derrick Morton, CEO of Seattle-based video game developer FlowPlay, says he leads a company where there are no bosses. No one reports to anyone else; they simply work in teams. "They need to be willing to take feedback and work with the group and not try and be a prima donna," he says. "I look at what their ego is like. How humble are they? They may be super talented, but if I don't get a sense of humbleness, they don't pass the test."[9]

A 2022 report by Universum says that collaboration ranks significantly higher than all the other desired employee attributes, including customer focus, problem solving, integrity/ethics, creativity, and drive. The reason it ranks #1 out of the 10 most in-demand characteristics is that the employers believe those who collaborate stay longer and work well in a hybrid environment.[10] You'll want to show how you've collaborated.

Don't use a tone of voice that sounds like bragging. Refrain from statements that use too many "I"s, as in "I did this" and "I did that." Give credit to others you worked with. When hiring for my firm, The Humphrey Group, I was always conscious of how many times candidates used "I" in their emails or during a face-to-face interview. There is no magic formula for how many "I"s should be used in your job script, but if you overdose on them, the hiring manager will not be impressed.

Unak notes that people with clout don't use "I" excessively. The company's AI finds that most people in job interviews talk more about themselves than about others. They frequently use *I, me, my, mine,* or *myself.* But according to Unak, "those with clout communicate by shifting the focus from themselves to the group they belong to. They frequently use words like *we, us, our, ours, ourselves.*"[11]

Bring others into your script and acknowledge their contributions, even when discussing your own. Interviewers know that few people in an organization complete a major project by themselves. Say, "I loved being part of a team that was so focused on results. Together we achieved more than any of us had imagined." Give credit to your mentors as well. Showing how you worked with others to succeed will impress the interviewer. Brendan Castle, head of recruiting for Google, tells candidates: "I like to see how you would include other people's thoughts and ideas as part of your problem-solving process especially if you're having difficulty coming up with a solution."[12]

You can still use "I," but add to it "we," "our team," "our partners," and others who made your achievements possible.

#8 Respect

Standout candidates show respect for others and for their companies of choice. Show respect with simple courtesies: show up on time for meetings and interviews, and keep your commitments. If you have promised to send someone your resume before you meet on Zoom, do it! No excuses.

Show respect by doing your research in advance of any meeting. If anyone is generous enough to meet with you, take time to research them and their company ahead of the meeting. Read everything you can about that firm, its culture, and the person you're meeting with. You can then sprinkle into the conversation observations that show you've done your research.

Show respect by using respectful language. Casual language is rampant in the office, and words such as "hey," "how's it going?" "100 percent," and "you guys" are standard fare. But during the job-seeking process, these expressions can create the impression that you are not taking the interviewer seriously or that you are getting too chummy. Avoid such informal language and keep the tone professional.

Show respect for everyone, regardless of rank. Zappos, a Las Vegas–based company, often offers job candidates a shuttle ride from the airport. The interview starts the second the candidate is in the shuttle and continues when they arrive at the front desk. Both shuttle drivers and front desk staff are asked to report on the conduct of candidates. If a potential employee is not pleasant to the driver or front desk rep, the company looks askance at that lack of respect.[13]

Finally, show respect in your answers to questions. Mark Unak told me that when he was CTO of Harqen, the company's analysis of interviews concluded that the single most important question in any job interview is "Why do you want to work for us?" Your answer can determine your fate.[14] Make sure to do your research and, using that information, show how much you admire the company, its business, and the role you wish to play.

#9 Gratitude

Few qualities are more important than gratitude. We humans crave appreciation, and showing gratitude will make you more appealing to those who hire and make *you* feel happier. Yes, studies show that when we express gratitude, we activate regions of our brain that release dopamine and serotonin—known as our "bliss" neurochemicals.[15]

Securing that next career position usually requires help—lots of it. Be sure to thank everyone who supports you along the way. I helped a job candidate with his resume, and he wrote me a note that touched my heart. It read (in part): "Oh my, Judith. None of this would have been possible without your help. You have worked hard on this, and most importantly, your blessing toward landing me a job that I wish for is immensely valuable."

Who should you thank?

Thank everyone who has supported you in your job journey. See chapter 11 for sample scripts you can use for thank-you notes.

As you craft your scripts for each stage in your job search, think about these nine characteristics that will enable you to make a strong impression. Whether you are writing a networking script, a resume, a cover letter, or answers to questions for an interview, use these expressions to create the kind of character you want to project. They will serve you well and show your attractiveness as a candidate.

Next, let's talk about the overarching message you want to have for your entire job search and for each episode in your journey.

CHAPTER 3

What's Your Message?

EVERY GOOD STORY HAS A consistent point of view, and so should yours.

You've decided on the kind of job you want, whether you want to stay with your present company or find a new job outside it, and the qualities you want to project. Now you need a message—something that will deliver a clear idea of who you are, what you want, and why someone should hire you. Looking for a job without a point is quite simply pointless. But you'll succeed in your search when it has unity and coherence. That singleness of purpose means that you'll want a strong, clear, and consistent message about yourself that energizes you and energizes every one of your scripts—from start to finish. This chapter shows why telling your story well requires an overarching message.

The Need for a Message

Your journey might begin with a networking event, or with an elevator pitch, or a Zoom conversation with an influencer. Or it could start with a casual encounter at your firm. It includes written submissions, so you'll want to develop a strong resume and customize it for each job you apply for. And you'll need a killer cover letter that explains why you believe you're a fit for the job.

Another hurdle comes when you're called in for interviews, whether in-person or by video. You'll need to prepare for challenging Q&As and even for oddball questions. You must be at your best no matter how many interviews you have. These can be with recruiters, hiring managers, team members, internal clients, and your future boss. It can seem like a grueling process.

This is the road to success—or so you hope. But it's a road paved with preparation. To move forward and get hired, you'll need a narrative that inspires. Each of these episodes in your job journey will require a script. This book will show you exactly how to create these inspiring narratives. If you want your actions over the course of many months to culminate in success, they must be unified. That's why your overall message is so important.

The Role of a Message

To stand out in today's highly competitive job market, you'll want to come across as a person who believes in yourself and who can inspire others to believe in you, too. Fundamental to this process is having a strong, clear, and consistent message about yourself that will energize every one of your scripts— absolutely everything, from start to finish. You need to be telling your story, and at the heart of a good story is a message that will get across your value.

There are two reasons for having a message that inspires.

First, it will ground you and give you confidence. I once had a client who was head of marketing for a major corporation. She was often in meetings with the executive team and the board of directors. She was frankly unsettled by being in these senior gatherings, perhaps because she was new to the firm and the only woman. To bolster her confidence, she had a message she repeated to herself every time she was headed for a senior leadership meeting. She'd say, "I am the head of marketing for a global technology organization." She'd repeat it silently over and over again until the meeting began. This was her mantra, her security blanket. And it worked. She spoke confidently and was promoted to CEO.

If you develop a one-sentence message at the beginning of your job search, you can deliver it to yourself—either fully or in an abbreviated form—and it will center you on the one thing that makes you exceptional and right for the jobs you are seeking. Knowing that will give you inner strength.

The second reason to have a self-defining message is that it will be the key idea you can deliver to everyone you meet. Whether you're networking, writing your resume, or walking into an interview, you will have an inspiring message about yourself that will explain your readiness for that next big job.

You want everyone to know that *one big thing* about you that will captivate them. You want to stay focused on that single message about yourself that you can commit to and convince others of. It will be adapted for each situation, but it should be a single idea about what you bring to that next assignment. It will keep you focused on the jobs that are right for you.

This message should be powerful and grounded in your particular strengths. Nobody will care about you if you say, "I am purpose driven" or "I am a self-starter" or "I like to work on my own." These vague, generic statements will not get you results, whether you use them in a networking conversation or an interview. Amanda Luthra, a senior recruiter, told me: "I find job candidates tell me things that they think I want to hear. They might say 'I'm goal driven,' or 'I'm a great communicator.' I find there is often this wall, and people are not letting me see who they really are."[1] What you want is one compelling idea that positions you for that next role. It will tell others whether you have the background, skills, character, passion, and vision to attain the goals you have in mind.

In the absence of such an inspiring and deeply felt message, networking contacts, recruiters, and interviewers will be left to draw their own conclusion about you. Do you want them to conclude that you are a techie when they want a leader? Or worse still, that they don't know what to make of you at all?

A clear, strong message is your secret superpower.

How to Develop Your Message

Craft this message by thinking about the answers you came up with during your self-reflection. Then, sit down and record yourself explaining how your career has taken shape and what the trajectory of that career is. You might pretend to be answering the question, "Tell me about yourself."

If you are a marketing professional, your first cut at a message might sound like this: "I have a passion for marketing, and in a series of increasingly senior positions, I have grown market share for three successive firms. I did this by having a keen sense of every market we entered and developing a strategic marketing plan, and it all worked. Now I'm ready for a senior role."

If you're a newbie applying for your first job, your initial cut might sound like this: "I have a math degree and a strong love of coding. In university, I was a winner in a competition that showed my proficiency in this field. And I am proud to be a female coder, looking for an assignment in what has traditionally been a male world."

Suppose you're applying for a position within your present company. Your message might be: "I'm looking to advance in our marketing department, having had a strong track record in my present role. I believe in this company and want to build my career in it."

Now see if you can shrink these messages to one sentence each. By developing one clear sentence, you'll have something that is easy to deliver—and memorable.

For example, the first candidate might compress her message to this one sentence: "I am a seasoned marketing leader with strong market intelligence and a track record to prove it."

The second young candidate might have as her message: "I love coding, have won awards for it, and am proud to be a female coder."

And the third: "I'm looking to advance in our marketing department and build upon my strong performance."

Putting your career—whether long or short—into one succinct sentence can be challenging because, increasingly, our careers do not follow a smooth trajectory. Even a seemingly consistent career can have twists and turns and may zigzag from one area of competency to another. Or your career may have gaps or include diverse fields of interest. But having a one-sentence message that inspires is critical. It's like a thesis in a term paper: it is your argument, the one thing you want to prove.

As you develop your message, find a thread that runs through all your jobs, which might begin with college and end with the job you now have. Or, if you have a long and distinguished career, you may want to go back only 15 years or so. If you are doing two or three different jobs now—say you have a freelance job on the side of a company position—make sure you explain how they are connected. If they don't fit, focus on the one that matters.

The important thing is to create an inspiring one-sentence message that defines your career strength and your readiness for the group of jobs you are pursuing.

Burn this message in your mind and have it ready at all times. It will strengthen your resolve to find just the right job. And when you deliver it to others, it will strengthen their commitment to you.

Customizing Your Message

The beauty of this one idea is that it can be adapted and customized for all your individual scripts. It won't be exactly the same in all your encounters, but as you use it again and again, it will create thematic continuity in your search.

Suppose your message is this: "I am a seasoned HR professional with a strong track record building employee engagement in three companies."

For a quick elevator pitch, your message might sound like this: "I do employee engagement really well."

You might customize this message for a networking conversation as follows: "I'd appreciate your helping me find a senior HR position that builds on my background in employee engagement."

The summary at the top of your resume might feature this customized version of your message: "A seasoned HR professional with a strong multicompany track record of creating employee programs that exceeded expectations, raised engagement, and increased retention."

You could begin a video interview with this customized message (and opening hook): "I am excited about this position. I'm a seasoned HR professional with a strength in employee engagement, and I know I'd succeed in this role."

In a live interview, you would want this message to sound more conversational: "I've got a strong HR background in employee engagement and would love to bring this expertise to the role we are discussing." You might add: "I believe this is what you are looking for."

This last sentence would be based on the candidate's research that shows the company needs employee engagement because it is facing retention problems.

Your Message Creates Consistency

All these versions of your message will serve you well as you script yourself throughout your job search. Using a single message, with appropriate examples, will focus your narrative. These iterations of your message are strong, clear, one-sentence statements that focus your pitch and show those you're communicating with that you have a clear sense of yourself and your value. They are so much better than the alternatives we often see (and that you may have been taught to concoct in the past). Too many messages take the form of overcrowded, jargon-filled statements, or there may be a total absence of any message at all.

The defining message will also focus your search. We hear again and again about candidates who apply for 50, 100, 200, even 400 jobs. This becomes a game of darts: the candidate keeps throwing that dart at the job board until something—anything—turns up. This is a terrible way to script yourself. Not only is it a waste of your time to apply all over the place, but if you're not focused, you won't create a winning narrative. Recruiters and companies will see that, and they'll reject your application. And the more rejections you get, the more discouraged you justifiably will be.

Your message will focus you on who you are, what you bring, and what select positions are right for you. Having a single message will also give coherence to your overall job journey. With the continuity of a single message, you won't think of delivering your elevator pitch, networking script, and interview script as disconnected events. They will be chapters in your saga that have the same messaging.

The pitch you make to a networking contact should leave that individual with the same conclusion about you that an interviewer might have at the end of an interview. Even though your resume likely will pass through the ATS system (particularly if you are applying externally), your defining message should pass muster with the bot if it is written in simple, straightforward prose.

How do you know if you have achieved this consistency? If someone heard you deliver your elevator pitch, heard your networking conversation, saw your resume, or was a fly on the wall during your interview, they would be able to say: "Ah, this is the same person." Your communications throughout should be that similar. The self-reflection that we talked about in chapters

1 and 2 will enable you to develop that single, centered profile of yourself. You'll then be able to take that message with you throughout your job journey. Its impact? Inspiring both you and your audience. Take time at the beginning of your job search to come up with that one powerful message.

Once you have that message, you need a structure that develops it. That's the subject of our next chapter, where you'll discover a template for creating every single script in your job journey.

CHAPTER 4

Script Yourself with HIRE

HAVING YOUR MESSAGE IN MIND is the beginning of developing your story. But you'll also need to know how to create scripts for each encounter. One of the biggest mistakes job seekers make is not preparing what they'll say. Some job candidates may be reluctant to write out notes for upcoming meetings or interviews because they don't want to sound too scripted or too wooden. But without a script you risk sounding unfocused.

The unscripted job candidate may ramble on, jumping from one idea to another, without the coherence or focus that drives home a point. One job seeker, Emily Moore, confessed her difficulties in her blog. She was rehearsing in front of her boyfriend for a job at Glassdoor, and he suddenly stopped her, exclaiming: "You're trying to cover too much."

She admitted: "There were so many different points I wanted to touch on—my previous roles, my skills, my accomplishments, my alma mater, my work style—that I blathered on and on to cover them all in the mock interviews I did with my boyfriend."[1]

Crowded, disorganized narratives leave a poor impression on networking contacts, recruiters, hiring managers—and even boyfriends! While you may not realize you're rambling, the interviewer will and will likely strike you from the list of desirable candidates. They'll be thinking, "this candidate is disorganized," or "she hasn't done her homework," or "*what* is he saying?"

In this chapter, you'll learn the fundamentals of creating scripts that deliver strong, clear, persuasive messages. The secret is the HIRE template. Use it, and you will be able to craft compelling scripts for every stage of your job search—elevator conversations, networking discussions, interviews, answers to questions, and even written documents like resumes and cover letters. Here is the four-part HIRE template for structuring all your scripts:

Hook—with a grabber
Inspire—with your message
Reinforce—with proof points
Engage—with a call to action

How to Use the HIRE Template

The secret to using this template is to understand the purpose of each of its four components—and how, together, they persuade the listener in every script.

HOOK (REACH OUT TO YOUR AUDIENCE)

The first component of the scripting template is a *hook* (the H in HIRE) that reaches out to your audience. It can also be thought of as a grabber or a verbal handshake. It captures the attention of your listener and builds a bridge to that person.

A simple hook might be, "Thank you for taking time to meet with me." If you are in an interview and your hiring manager says, "Tell me about yourself," your hook might be "I'd be glad to. Let me tell you about my career success." The examples in this book show you how to customize the hook for each occasion. You'll learn that there are certain ones not to use, like "Um," "Ah," "Let me think," or "That's a good question." All of those are common filler expressions. Avoid them.

INSPIRE (WITH YOUR MESSAGE)

The second component of the scripting template should *inspire* (the I in HIRE). This is your compelling message, the one point you want to make. It's your *why*. For example, in an internal interview, your inspiring idea might be, "This position is the ideal next step in my career with this company," or "I'm excited about the seasoned leadership I'd bring to this role." Or you might inspire with a cover letter message like this: "My experience, passion, and track record have led me to this position." You'll find abundant examples of inspiring messages in this book.

REINFORCE (WITH PROOF POINTS)

The third component of your scripting template should reinforce your message with proof points that are numbered. Because they *reinforce* the message, they are the R in HIRE. There are several ways to structure your proof points. Here are three patterns to choose from.

The first option is *chronological.* Let's say your message in a job interview is, "I'm an excellent candidate for this position since, during the past 10 years, I've delivered strong results as an HR manager." You'd choose this chronological pattern:

1. From 2011–2014 I headed HR at Devco Housing and raised employee satisfaction during a period when the company underwent a major restructuring.

2. In my next job, which I held from 2015 to 2018, I was HR lead for a pharma company and introduced a series of wellness programs that were embraced by employees.

3. In my most recent position, I oversaw talent recruitment and helped bring top talent to our firm.

A second way to structure your proof points is to make them *reasons that reinforce* your message. For example, if your message is, "I'm passionate about marketing," your proof points might be the reasons you say that:

1. I really "get" marketing.
2. I'm a big believer in market research.
3. I've expanded the market reach of my present company, with big sales figures.

A third approach is to have two proof points: one describing a *situation* and the other describing a *response.* Let's say you're asked about a problem you solved, and your message is, "I turned around a problem situation with our largest client, and the payoff was huge." To reinforce this main idea, first describe the situation you faced, and then your response:

1. Our major client threatened to leave because they felt their technology needs were not being addressed by our product line.

2. I listened carefully to their demands and responded fully—sustaining a relationship with a payoff of $5 million a year.

Look at your message and ask yourself which of these three patterns will best reinforce your message.

ENGAGE (WITH A CALL TO ACTION)

The fourth component of your scripting template *engages* (the E in HIRE) with a call to action that suggests next steps. At the end of a job interview with your boss, you might say: "I am excited about this opportunity and feel I'm worthy to take on this assignment." In a networking conversation, your close may be asking for a meeting or requesting that person send your resume to the hiring manager. Occasionally, you'll speak about the next steps you—or both you and your listener—will take: "I'll send you my resume and look forward to hearing from you."

The HIRE template will allow you to create a compelling story every step of the way. When you use it, you'll have an easy-to-remember approach to designing your scripts, and you'll distinguish yourself from job seekers who speak without a message or have so many points they appear to have none. You'll be a standout job seeker who creates a positive impression in all your exchanges. Quite simply, you'll get hired with HIRE.

An Example Using the HIRE Template

To see how brilliantly the HIRE template can serve you in crafting job scripts, look at this example, which shows the "bones" of a candidate's interview script.

Hook—with a grabber
I've spent the past four years working in the tech industry, and I am looking to bring my expertise to a new organization like yours.

Inspire—with your message
I have gotten results working in a fast-paced environment that encourages drive and success.

Reinforce—with proof points
1. Business results: I've doubled my line of business in the past 24 months.

2. Team results: I've led several cross-functional working teams to drive projects through to completion.

3. Cultural results: I play an active role in our company's diversity and inclusion efforts and lead an employee resource group with global employee participation.

Engage—with a call to action
I would love to walk you through my interpretation of a business challenge you are facing and how I would help you overcome it.

The HIRE template is an enormously powerful tool for any job seeker. You can use it to structure all your job scripts. And, as you can see from this example, it will give you the power to persuade. If you're faced with an impromptu situation—a question comes at you that you didn't expect—you can also use this template on the fly.

Fleshing Out the Script

The outline in the previous section is a skeleton of a good script, the bare bones. You'll need to add content. Your hook may be a one-liner, but it could be longer. If you're meeting with an interviewer, you might begin: "Hello, thank you for this meeting. I've long admired your company, and when I saw this job advertised, I immediately decided to apply." Your inspiring message should always be one sentence—and only one. For example, "This is my dream job, and I believe it's a great fit with my background." You may have between two and four reinforcing points, and each likely will be developed with examples and stories. Engage at the end of your script with one sentence or several. But make sure whatever content you add amplifies your points and doesn't pull away from them.

• • •

The HIRE template is your secret weapon for telling your story and landing that job. Nobody will know you're using it, but you'll sound and be inspiring when you do.

This structural model underpins every script in this book, and it is equally useful for internal job searches as for external pitches. Use HIRE, and you'll project clear thinking. You'll be well on your way to distinguishing yourself as a candidate who deserves to land your dream job. But you'll want to do more than have a script in your head. You'll want to deliver it like a pro, which brings us to rehearsing.

CHAPTER 5

Rehearse, Rehearse, Rehearse

TO SUCCEED IN YOUR JOB JOURNEY, you'll need to deliver your scripts with clarity and confidence. You'll want to bring energy and enthusiasm to your performance. Don't wait until the interview to learn your lines. Write out what you want to say, and then practice those lines.

I've always devoted an extraordinary amount of time to preparing for every speaking event. You'll never know how good your script is until you practice it—and get feedback from others. I once wrote a whopping 14 drafts of a speech I was to deliver at a dinner given in my honor. For each draft, I rehearsed with a different person—many of them actors who knew how to bring a script to life. That was time well spent, and that night I was able to shine. You, too, want to shine in every encounter.

Whether you're preparing for a job interview with a new company or pitching yourself to your boss for an elevated position, you want to be well rehearsed. You should even prepare for networking meetings. Practice with the following guidelines in mind.

Be "In" the Script

The starting point of a great delivery is making sure *you* are in the script. What you say must reflect the story of who you are and what you believe you can offer. Any book on acting will tell you that you have to be in character. The fact that you are the scriptwriter means you have the power to create a story that's meaningful to you and that portrays you as the best candidate for the job.

Ask yourself: Is this me talking? Have I fully shown my readiness for the new role? Am I presenting myself as the strong candidate I want to be? Would I hire me for this job? If so, bravo. You are ready to move on and learn your lines. If not, tweak the text. Edit the lines that don't work. See if everything reflects your strong beliefs about yourself and what you are capable of. For example, suppose the script you've prepared for an interview says, "I am a hard worker." You might look at that line and say to yourself, "Well, I don't know if I want to cast myself that way. I am more than that. 'I perform at a high level' might be better, or 'I complete projects on time and with great success.'" Own the words.

Make sure the script sounds genuine and conversational. Avoid language or sentence patterns that are too formal. I came across one such example in an answer recommended by a career site. The interview question was: "Why are you interested in this position?" Here was the suggested response: "The first thing that caught my eye when I saw the position posted was definitely that it was at EFG Advisers. I know that you build a lot of your tools in-house, that the team is small, and you run a variety of long- and short-term strategies in the US equities markets using a quantitative approach."[1]

The sentences in this answer are too long and don't sound authentic. The first sentence has 21 words, and the second is 36 words. Most sentences we speak are much shorter. Break up your long sentences.

To achieve an authentic style, read what you've written out loud. Speaking out loud will lead you to a simpler version. Michael Palombo, who was hired into a senior role at Twitter, tells me when he was preparing for his job interview, he took the time to make his script his own. As he explains: "I'll usually write out the entire script, walk away, come back and read it out loud, several times. That way, I can make sure it sounds natural. I'll do some editing to get rid of any stiffness in the language and make sure it sounds like me."[2]

The Silent Rehearsal

The next step, once you have a script you like, is to internalize it.

Find a quiet place and mentally review the script. Focus on the structural components. Think about why you chose that particular hook, whether your message inspires, how well your proof points support your argument, and whether you truly engage your audience with your call to action. Your delivery will emphasize that structure.

Run through the entire script by yourself in silence, and deliver it to yourself until you can do so without looking at the paper. Suppose you have an important networking conversation coming up the next day. You've written out your remarks using the HIRE template. Take a half-hour to learn the script. The advantage of doing this is that you'll deliver with more certainty. The words will flow because they are clear in your mind. You will bring the script to life for your audience. This will create an energetic, inspiring performance. The same process applies when you're getting ready for a big job interview. You'll want to review and master your interview script. One millennial job applicant, Noah Yashinsky, told me how hard he worked to prepare for a key Amazon interview.

"How did you learn your script?" I asked.

"Through repetition," he told me. "I would practice and practice, to the point where I could deliver a lot of the content off the cuff. I prepared for three weeks, and learning the script was the culmination of the process."[3] He landed the job.

Mastering your script is very different from memorizing it. Michael Palombo says: "I'll internalize the script. What I try to stay away from is memorizing it verbatim. Memorizing can really trip you up because if you forget a word, there is a higher risk of blanking out. So, I prefer internalizing sound bites."[4]

As you're learning the text, certain phrases will stick with you. That's useful. But don't try to learn the script word-for-word. The goal in mastering your script is to learn the flow of your ideas—the narrative you have created. That well-structured script will give clarity and strength to your talk.

And it's all worth it. If you want the job badly, you must turn in your best performance. Learn your script through this silent and dedicated practice.

How do I know this technique works? I've used it myself.

In the many years while I was building The Humphrey Group, I'd write a brief script before every sales call and get it down cold. I remember often sitting in my car in a client's parking lot, learning my script just before walking into the building. I'd be saying to myself things like: "So good to meet you, I've heard so much about you. Our executive speaking program is designed for top leaders like you" and "Here are the reasons I know it will meet your needs." Before I left the car I'd conclude with, "I know this program will help you, and I look forward to working with you." The parking attendant may have wondered why I was sitting there so long after I'd arrived, but it didn't matter. I was fully prepped—I was on fire!

I loved pitching because I knew this approach made me a strong influencer. And it also gave me the confidence to listen and ask questions. When you know what you are going to say, you have more insight into what questions to ask. As counter-intuitive as it sounds, the more prepared you are, the better a listener you become.

Once you've learned the flow of your text, you're free to concentrate on the interpersonal dimension of the exchange: free to listen, free to ask questions, and free to deliver your powerful thinking without tentativeness (the *ums* and *ahs*).

For the Big Events: Rehearse Out Loud

Practicing quietly is excellent, but when you have an important meeting with an influencer, recruiter, or hiring executive, it's best to rehearse out loud. Practice delivering in front of a coach, friend, or family member. You can also record yourself with your phone or computer, so you can review your delivery and analyze it.

Noah Yashinsky said when he was preparing for his highly successful Amazon interviews—five in one day—he practiced out loud in front of a whole series of family members, parents, uncles, aunts, anyone who would listen and give him feedback.[5]

And it worked! He was totally "on" in the interviews and won over his interviewers. In rehearsing out loud—in front of others or for your own playback—you'll have valuable feedback on the quality of your delivery.

Here are the key aspects of your practice that you should focus on.

#1 YOUR ENERGY AND ENTHUSIASM

Make sure your voice is full of energy and conveys enthusiasm and conviction. This shows the interviewer that you are excited about the opportunity you're discussing. Bring the strongest expression to your main points: your message and supporting reasons. For example, if your message is, "I'm an excellent candidate for this job because of my strong background in media relations and executive communications," punch out these words. You'll also want to emphasize the structural signposts for each reason. These signposts can be "first," "second," and "third." Or "to begin with," "in addition," and "finally."

Emphasize the important verbs. A typical interview script might include the following action words: "meet," "admire," "impressed," "perform," "lead," and "oversee." Bring those phrases to life with energy and conviction.

#2 YOUR PACE

As you practice, don't rush. Controlling your speed in your practice session will help you maintain an unhurried pace in your interview. Speeding up is a mistake that candidates sometimes make because they're nervous. Take your time with each statement. Pause before answering questions. Don't fill that pause with "uh," "ah," "let me think," or "that's a good question." Instead, pause in silence. Show that you are taking the question seriously and giving yourself time to reflect on it.

As you speak, vary your pace. If you deliver every sentence at the same speed, you'll bore the listener. Slow down for the important statements (main points, concluding statements, key ideas), and pick up your pace when delivering stories or anecdotes that should be presented with a bit more ease and flow.

Learn the power of the pause, and pause longer than you think you should at the end of sentences or sentence groups. Stopping between thoughts strengthens the impression you make. It shows you want to give your audience (and yourself) time to think about what you are saying. Your audience can't process an idea until you have delivered it. The pauses give your listeners time to do that.

#3 YOUR BODY LANGUAGE

As you rehearse, use body language to reinforce your enthusiasm and conviction. Make sure you have a warm, enthusiastic expression on your face—but don't smile all the time, or that will weaken the impression you're creating. Be sure to look at your audience when you are speaking. If you're practicing for a Zoom interview, make sure the camera is positioned so you are looking directly at your interviewer.

Keep your body still, but not stiff. Try not to fidget. It makes you look nervous. Stillness is power. Movement is best expressed by gestures. Keep your arms open and gesture with full arms, not wrists or elbows. Movement from the wrists or elbows looks less confident. Full arm gestures will allow you to demonstrate that you are physically reaching out to the other person. If you're preparing for a Zoom session, make sure your gestures are visible but not overwhelming. You should sit far enough away from your laptop so that your upper body shows and the tops of your arms show when you are gesturing. Don't sit so far back that your whole body is visible.

As you rehearse, ask those observing you to check that you are on track with these delivery techniques. (You can also check up on your body language by recording yourself on video.) Benefit from the feedback you get and keep practicing—you'll be great.

• • •

I have set the bar high in urging you, my readers, to perfect your scripts and practice for a strong delivery. My advice assumes you'll have the time, space, resources, and physical and mental readiness to prepare "perfectly." But that won't always be the case. You may get a call out of the blue. Schedules may change, and you may not be feeling up to the challenge. Don't worry! Life is full of surprises, and we can't always be perfect. In fact, organizational psychologist Adam Grant put it well when he said: "desire for perfection is a recipe for burnout." He urges us to strive for "good enough."[6] Do your best, but don't worry if circumstances mean you're not 100 percent ready.

If there's an accommodation you need due to a disability or health issue, I encourage you to ask for it. Not only will this help you succeed in the interview, you'll also gain insight into the employer's policies. A hiring company willing to make such an accommodation is committed to inclusion and would be a great place to work.

Interviewing for a new job can be stressful. But remember that in each encounter, you're learning about the company just as they are finding out about you. Do your best to prepare—but also make sure you find the organization that's the best fit for you.

PART II

CONVERSATIONAL SCRIPTS

As a job seeker, your journey often begins with the informal conversations you have with colleagues, networking contacts, mentors, sponsors, and bosses. In Part II of this book, you will discover how to develop an elevator pitch that captures your listener's attention. You'll also learn how to script yourself for successful networking encounters and how to promote yourself to the right people when you want to rise within your present company. These are all informal but critical conversations.

CHAPTER 6

Crafting Your Elevator Pitch

THE JOB MARKET IS ALL ABOUT SELLING yourself, and there is no better sales tool than a good elevator pitch. Despite its name, this is not a script designed just for elevator chats.

Its role is much broader than that. It is the pitch that allows you to get your point across in brief encounters. Those encounters can be make-or-break situations for job seekers. You'll need this kind of script when you're telling a friend you're looking for that next big job, when you're with a key person at a networking event, when you're talking to HR about a job in your company, or when you run into a neighbor who might provide you with a job lead. In short, you'll need a pithy pitch for those brief and often spontaneous encounters when you want to describe yourself as a credible job seeker.

Having an elevator script for your career conversations will focus your thinking, demonstrate your value, and save you from delivering messages about yourself that are too general or too scattered. It's your go-to script when networking with influencers or pitching yourself informally. It's far more concise than any speech—30 seconds is about the right length. But it has all the same elements as a longer talk. It begins with a *hook* (or grabber) that reaches out to the audience, then *inspires* with a message, *reinforces* the message with proof points, and finally *engages* with "next steps." It is your best approach for early-stage conversations when looking for a job.

Always Have It in Your Back Pocket

While you won't use an elevator pitch for every situation, having one in your back pocket means you'll have a quick script to use when you suddenly find yourself explaining who you are and what you do. If you don't have that script, you may be in trouble.

A Gen Z intern I know, within seconds of walking into a company cafeteria, spotted a manager who had advertised a position this young man wanted. His internship was coming to an end, and this opportunity, he thought, would be the perfect next step for him. He confidently walked over to this manager and began a conversation.

"I understand you are looking for a junior software developer," he said.

"Yes, we are," the manager said. "Are you interested?"

He responded "yes"—and then he froze. He hadn't thought it through and couldn't collect his thoughts. He was speechless. Instead of creating an opportunity, this chance encounter in the cafeteria created a full stop. The young man didn't approach this hiring manager again. He never got the job.

Having an elevator pitch prepared will serve you well in such chance encounters. If the employee in this story had already thought through why he was right for this position, he might have replied: "Yes, I believe I'd be a good fit with this role because I have a computer science degree and proficiency in Python and JavaScript. I'd love to have a meeting with you about it."

I once delivered an elevator script to the head of HR of a high-tech company. I knew what I wanted to say, wrote it out in note form, and kept it to 30 seconds. Then I placed a call (after hours, when I thought he'd be answering his own phone). Lo and behold, he did answer. There was a moment of trembling, but I found my voice.

The elevator script I delivered changed my life. Here it is:

"Hello, this is Judith Humphrey. I have noticed several recent ads for positions in your company, and I wonder if you'd be interested in hiring someone with my experience. I have an MA in English and have taught communications at York University for the past eight years. I developed a program for instructors, who now teach writing as part of their courses. I know Northern Telecom is a great believer in good communications, and I'd love to be considered for a position."

The head of HR liked what he heard and booked a meeting for me with the senior vice president of corporate relations, who hired me. That short elevator pitch got me into the business world, where I have had a richly rewarding career.

In your job journey, you'll need to use elevator scripts for planned and unplanned situations. For example, you'll want one for networking situations or when meeting a recruiter at a job fair. Elevator pitches can also take a written form, such as introducing yourself to a LinkedIn contact. This brief narrative sells you and your worth in any short professional encounter.

More generally, the ability to craft a compelling elevator pitch is an important skill for advancing at every stage of your career. It focuses your response when a boss wonders why you should be given a specific project or when a client asks you, "Why should we hire you?" These short bursts of personal PR will fast forward your career.

Scripting Your Elevator Pitch

The elevator pitch must be flexible—one size does not fit all. It's customized for each situation, but in every case, it draws upon your personal value proposition. It shows what you can add to a company that makes you such a special hire. It highlights your experience without making you sound arrogant or pushy.

A good elevator pitch has a clear and persuasive design that uses the four-part HIRE template featured in this book. Here is how to build it:

Step 1: Begin with a hook that creates rapport with your audience. When speaking to an executive it might sound like this: "You know the retail industry inside and out, and I'd appreciate a few minutes of your time to learn more about opportunities." If you're talking to a recruiter about a specific position, your opening might be: "I'm looking forward to meeting you at the upcoming job fair. I've heard such good things about you." If you're approaching a colleague in HR you could begin: "I've found a job posting in your department, and I'd love your views on it."

Step 2: Inspire with a message. Whether you're applying for lots of positions or focused on a single opportunity, ask yourself the following questions when formulating your message.

- What will I bring to my next role?
- Why would I be a great fit in this new position?
- What strengths will I bring to my next employer?

Here are some messages you might come up with.

- I believe my background will enable me to lead market-ing to new heights.
- I'm confident I have what it takes to build sales in the advertised role.
- My strong track record in claims will be an asset.
- As CFO in three consulting firms, I bring strong indus-try experience.

Notice a few things about these key ideas. They position the candidate as a person who has been successful. They sug-gest that pertinent experience will enable the candidate to be a high achiever in the new job. And the language is confident: no caveats (possibly, maybe), no tentative verbs (I think, I feel, I might), no filler words (um, ah, well). Your ability to inspire is the soul of your elevator pitch. It is conveyed in the one-sen-tence message you want to get across to everyone. You'll use it again and again. And you'll customize it for each situation. But it can't stand all by itself. It must be developed, which takes us to the next step.

Step 3: Reinforce your message with proof points. You might provide reasons.

1. My track record includes administering our benefits program.
2. I was also involved in designing an employee satisfaction program.
3. I've led a team of 12, and we have surpassed all our targets.

If you've had a series of positions, you might instead reinforce chronologically, showing how you've built your credentials from one job to the next.

1. After graduating, I was fortunate to find a position with a team leader who taught me a lot about HR practices.

2. In my next job, I applied what I learned and implemented three new HR policies.

3. I'm now leading a team of HR professionals.

Still another approach for organizing these proof points would be the situation/response model. You might sketch in the opportunity as you see it, then explain why your credentials represent a great fit.

Step 4: Engage with a call to action. This can be the toughest part of your elevator script because it is an ask. If you are talking to an influencer who works in the firm you're applying to, you might engage by asking that person to provide a reference or make a phone call on your behalf. If you're closing off a job interview conversation with a recruiter, engage by saying, "I'm looking forward to next steps. When can I expect to hear from you?" If you're talking to a career counselor at the beginning of your search, you might say, "I believe I have the credentials to provide the leadership XYZ company is looking for. I'll await your guidance on next steps."

That's the four-step HIRE template for building a compelling elevator pitch.

Delivering Your Elevator Pitch

Once you've created this brief talk, you're ready to practice and deliver it. Suppose you're interested in working with a career coach and you want to ask her on the phone if she'll help you. Your call might sound like this:

Hook—with a grabber
I am calling because I'm looking for a job and you come highly recommended.

Inspire—with a message
I have a strong track record as an HR professional
in the retail sector and am ready to make my
next big move.

Reinforce—with proof points
1. My background includes building an employee wellness program.

2. I have also led retail teams that have earned accolades.

3. I'm now looking for a senior HR role in retail that will take me to the next level.

Engage—with next steps
I'd love to know how we might work together. My
number is . . .

If you were delivering this script as part of a live interaction, your script won't sound exactly like this. After all, the person you're speaking to will interject comments. For example, she might say, "I understand," "That sounds great," or "Are you actively looking for a job?" You'll have to respond to these comments and questions. But your script will shape the conversation and get to your end point. You'll stay on message. You'll make your case well and point to next steps. This is what's called taking control of the conversation. If you don't, the other person will, or no one will. Neither of those outcomes spells success.

On-the-Fly Elevator Pitches

For situations like the one just mentioned, you can prepare your elevator script in advance. If you know you're going to a "meetup" or networking event or need to make a critical phone call, prepare your pitch. The more you do this, the better you'll be when it comes to creating on-the-fly elevator pitches. There are also many impromptu situations where you'll need to script yourself on the fly.

For example, suppose you're in a coffee shop and have a chance encounter with a neighbor. You happen to be looking for your next job, and you know this neighbor has a management position at a company where you'd like to get an interview. If you've mastered the art of the elevator script using the HIRE template, you'll be able to create a pitch on the fly. Here's how it might sound.

Hook—with a grabber
Hi Jaclyn [neighbor], how are you?

Thanks for asking. I'm doing well. How about you?

Great, thanks. Things are good at home, the kids are doing fine. And I'm actually on the job market.

Oh! I hope you'll find something you like.

Well, now that you mention it, I would love an introduction to Amazon. I wonder if you'd be kind enough to look at my resume.

I'd be happy to.

Inspire—with a message

I have a background that I believe would be a great fit.

Reinforce—with proof points

1. I've worked in Walmart's distribution centers.

2. As well, I've led teams in Costco's distribution centers, and

3. I know Amazon is hiring for its new warehouse in Toronto.

Engage—with a call to action

If I send you my resume, would you put in a good word for me?

Send it to me and I'll see what I can do.

Thank you so much!

Notice that the hook in this script is extended. In a casual situation, you don't want to rush your pitch; there may be a need for chitchat. But the job seeker in this example doesn't lose his way. He gets to his point—and develops it. If he hadn't mastered the art of the elevator conversation using HIRE, he wouldn't be able to create an impromptu script like the one here. Imagine how different the conversation could have been:

"What flavor coffee is that?"

Oh, I'm having a latte.

"Nice to see you. Say hi to your mom."

That's friendly chatter that goes nowhere!

The elevator pitch is the best way to break the ice and advance yourself, particularly in the very early stages of a job search or career conversation.

A pitch is crucial for networking and for encounters where you ask friends, colleagues, and business ties for help. You'll find, as in the creation of other scripts, that the HIRE template used here remains the all-important guide. Internalize that structure and master the ability to present your value proposition in these short bursts.

With any luck, delivering your elevator pitch will lead to a longer and more targeted networking conversation, which we'll explore next.

CHAPTER 7

Nailing the Networking Conversation

NETWORKING IS ALL ABOUT ASKING others for help. Doing so is a smart move when you're looking for a job. Research indicates that up to 85 percent of jobs come from networking. And 70 percent of jobs are not even advertised![1] Don't be shy about asking for help. But seeking support—especially from someone in a position of power—can be scary. I recently met with a young, fresh-out-of-university job seeker who shared her fear of networking. She said she was afraid of "bothering" people in positions of authority. She thought they'd think she was presumptuous to call on them.

I told her that most people will admire her for her courage. They will be glad to assist if you approach them with the right attitude and if they are in a position to help. As Steve Jobs remarked, "I've never found anybody that didn't want to help me if I asked them for help." As a twelve-year-old, he cold-called Bill Hewlett, cofounder of Hewlett-Packard. That conversation led to a summer internship at HP and was the start of a stellar career.[2]

The secret to successful networking lies in building a strong circle of backers and inspiring those you ask to help. This chapter will show you how to create that network and how to design and deliver scripts that get the backing of influencers.

Building Your Network

Creating your network is a crucial first step. Don't wait until you are desperate to leave your present job—or decide you want to move up within your company. Expand your circle now. Every career conversation you have with someone you know or meet—particularly someone who is able to help you—will reap returns when you are ready to make your move.

Let me give you an example.

A woman I know wasn't looking for a job, but she was networking anyway. When she was in the US for a holiday, she looked up a friend of a friend who worked for a global investment company. They chatted over coffee, and that was that . . . or so it seemed. A year later, when she found herself without a job, she reconnected with this senior finance leader.

She asked him if he knew of any job openings. He replied: "I hear there is one in wealth management working directly with clients. I suggest you apply." She did. He put in a good word for her. And after several interviews, she landed the job. If she hadn't done that original networking, she wouldn't have had that "in." One conversation with a stranger made all the difference.

Arranging a meeting to ask for guidance is also an excellent technique. You may have heard the adage, "Have a meeting to get advice, and you may end up with a job." That was true of several of the hires I made while I was CEO of The Humphrey Group. Here is an example.

The husband of one of our instructors came to me not for a job, but for information. He knew I'd been a speechwriter early in my career, and he wanted to move into speechwriting in the pharmaceutical world. He asked for advice about how to do that.

He had come through a family connection, so I listened closely. As he talked, I thought to myself, "This individual would be an asset to our company. He is so eloquent, so gracious and complimentary. He's done his research on me and our company. And he has moved me!"

I responded, "I am not that familiar with the world of pharma, but I can tell you that you'd be a great asset to our company. You are so well spoken and engaging as a communicator. I am inspired. Would you consider joining The Humphrey Group?" He looked at me in astonishment and said he would be honored. He'd just have to ask his wife if she'd mind having him as a colleague. She agreed, and he was a tremendous resource to our company for many years.

This is what I mean by inspire! He turned me into a believer. And how exactly did he do that? He came in well prepared to discuss his strengths. He also had great respect for our company, for my leadership, and for our success. According to career coach Tejal Wagadia, "When you approach someone for an informational interview, make it about them. Do your research, show respect for their tenure in a company or what they've accomplished in their career."[3]

Networking successfully takes time—but it delivers results. Start by building strong connections within your company. Target executives or senior leaders who would be able to influence your career by sponsoring you internally or heading a department you may want to work in. They would also be able to recommend you if you go outside the firm for your next job. To meet these influencers, attend company networking events or get involved in projects they may lead.

Keep your eye, too, on external networking opportunities. Joseph Testani, deputy to the president at University of Rochester and former director of the university's career center, advises that you take a comprehensive approach to networking: "Talk to your friends. Their families. Peers. Faculty members. Alumni. Recruiters. Even people you haven't spoken to in a few years. Ask questions and learn about them as people, idea-generators for careers, collaborators for start-ups, sources of volunteer opportunities, job leads, and references for graduate or professional school. Ask them for other people who may be fun or interesting to talk to, and if they would be open to make an introduction. It's a fast way to build a network. Make this a priority by dedicating 20 to 30 percent of your job search time to networking and connecting with others."[4]

Some experts suggest reaching out to one person a day while you are active in your search. But it's also important to grow your network even when you're not shopping for a new job. Steve Johnson, the head of Berkshire Grey, a firm that builds robotic systems, says, "I'll look at my calendar at the start of each week and search for a random empty slot or two I can fill by spending time with people I haven't seen in a while."

"Being deliberate about sustaining real relationships works," says Johnson. He's been keeping a list of friends, colleagues, and professors ever since college—and that list keeps growing. Every New Year, he sends a "simple message to old friends, former colleagues, or future coworkers."[5]

Joining professional associations can also help build your network. Once you join, volunteer for a committee or a high-profile project. Even though you may not be looking for a job yet, opportunities will come your way when you raise your profile. That was the case for me early in my career.

I got my third job through a professional association. I joined the International Association of Business Communicators and, soon after joining, launched a speechwriting course for IABC members in major North American cities. Someone from Shell Canada took my course and recommended me for a senior speechwriting job in her company. I was interviewed and got the job. It was a great assignment where I wrote speeches for the CEO. And when I started my own company, he introduced me to many other CEOs.

Another approach to networking is to reach out to individuals in companies or industries you are interested in working for. You don't have to know them. Introduce yourself and say, "I saw an article about you in the press. I see you're working at company XYZ, and I'd love to get your perspective on the organization, what you like, and what your experience has been." Email is an excellent way to contact these individuals.

Finally, use social media to expand your network. Connect with those in your industry and follow companies you may want to work for—ideally, they will follow you in return. LinkedIn is the best place to foster these business relationships. It gives you the opportunity to get to know those who might be able to help you get that coveted job or assignment in the future.

When you find a job that interests you, Tejal Wagadia recommends that you reach out on LinkedIn to the hiring manager or executive, particularly if the position is in a small or mid-sized company. As she explained to me: "If you've applied for an accounting position, connect with the senior manager in that area and message that individual. Say, 'I'm very impressed by your company and have applied for the advertised position. I wonder if you would be kind enough to answer a few questions I have.'"[6]

Six Categories of People to Include in Your Network

Some groups are crucial for your job search. Here are six you should reach out to.

COLLEAGUES

Look to your home base when building your network. Form strong ties with those in the organization where you work.

Early in my career, I joined a large bank and shortly after met with each of my direct reports. One of them gave me this advice: "Keep your head down." I asked what she meant. She explained, "Do your work, and don't get involved with the things around you. That way, any problems will just fly over your head." That was poor advice. In maintaining a low profile, she had no advocates, no colleagues who would vouch for her, and no conversations that would raise her profile. She was never promoted.

Keeping your head *up* is far better. Spend time talking with your colleagues, building relationships, and discovering your advocates. Show others you are an asset. Later you'll be able to call on them for help if you want to move up in the organization.

FRIENDS

Another source of assistance is your friends, particularly those who are well placed in the areas where you're job hunting. When speaking with them about opportunities, pitch yourself in a polished, professional way. Be purposeful, or you might end up reminiscing about good old times and fail to get to the point.

EXECUTIVES

A recommendation from someone in a high place is golden, but you'll only get one if you prepare well. When I founded The Humphrey Group, I often asked my CEO clients, "Do you know anyone else who would like this communications training?" Sure enough, they would give me two or three names of other C-level executives. I'd pitch those individuals, carefully preparing my script. I'd call them after 5 p.m., when their assistant would be gone and I could speak to them directly. I'd never leave a message expecting them to return the call. Plan what you'll say. If you're polite and to the point, they will likely be obliging.

HR PROFESSIONALS

Including HR managers and recruiters in your network is of great importance. You might encounter some of them at a job fair or a meet-and-greet event. Take time to think about how you'll position yourself with these gatekeepers. It's their business to put the right people in the right positions, but it's your job to put your best self forward. And don't wait until you want a job to approach a recruiter. As CEO of Korn Ferry, Gary Burnison, writes in his book *Lose the Resume, Land the Job*, "The best time to reach out to a recruiter is when you are already employed and not actively looking for a job."[7]

INDUSTRY INFLUENCERS

If you're interested in a particular industry, find out who in the industry might help you. One great way to reach these people is to go to their company websites and read their profiles. Do your research on them, see what they've accomplished, and then go to LinkedIn and message them. In 200 characters or less, tell them why you admire them and that you would appreciate their insight into how you might break into their industry or pursue your next career move in their industry or their company.

FAMILY MEMBERS

Those closest to you can be a source of support. A client of mine told me that her son, who had just graduated from university, wanted to work at the United Nations. She filled me in on his strong credentials. I happened to know an ambassador at the UN, and I made the connection. The ambassador introduced him to the very person he had dreamed of working for.

The starting point of networking is to have a robust network. All the avenues discussed here will give you a wealth of opportunities.

Preparing Your Networking Pitch

Once you've expanded your network, prepare an inspiring script for those you wish to approach. While some people are spontaneously eloquent, it's rare to be able to speak off the cuff in a way that inspires your listeners. Most people—even the best speakers—realize they have to prepare to be inspiring when speaking informally. As Mark Twain once said: "I never could make a good impromptu speech without several hours to prepare it."[8]

The same holds true for networking. Preparation is key. Just imagine yourself sitting in a room (or on a Zoom call) with an executive you barely know. In that brief meeting, you'll hope to gain a favorable response by winning her confidence. That's a lot of pressure. A prepared narrative will keep your confidence up in this potentially tense situation. Prepare a customized script for each encounter or each ask. Write it out, learn it, rehearse it, and make it flawless. Don't go to a meeting without it. And don't send an email or a voice mail to request a meeting until you have crafted a script.

If you don't prepare well, you may end up losing out on the assistance you're seeking. That lack of preparation was obvious in this voice mail a job seeker left for me (I've changed her name):

> Hi, this is Elizabeth Drew. Remember me (laugh). I was a friend of Anita's and came with her to your shoe party. Yeah, well, I'm looking for a job and I know you know a lot of people, so I would like a reference to anybody you know who might be in a sales organization . . . that's my background, though I started a business recently that I can tell you about. But I really want a job, I need the money. My number is . . . Looking forward to hearing from you.

This script is riddled with mistakes. First, it shouldn't have been left on voice mail—she should have called back until she got me or sent me an email. She doesn't sell herself well. She is presumptuous in her ask, saying, "remember me," when I had no recollection of her. She gives me absolutely no reason to want to help her. And she says she wants a job because she needs the money. She leaves it in my hands to call her back. I did call her back (she was a friend of a friend), but I didn't help her. To avoid messy calls like this one, *prepare*. You don't need a formal, memorized script, but you do need talking points that guide you. Learn them so well that you could deliver them in your sleep (or almost!).

If this job seeker had been unable to get me by phone, she could have sent this email:

Hello Judith,

We met at your lovely shoe party last fall. I'm now looking for a new job and would like to discuss any opportunities you may know of. I am a senior sales professional with 15 years of experience, and I am seeking a leadership role with a retail sales organization. Would you have time for a phone call or Zoom conversation in the next week or two? Thank you in advance for your support.

Best regards,
Elizabeth Drew

This script is inviting. She has a warm opening. She is clear about her background and her goals, and she comes across as a person worthy of my time and a possible reference. I would have met with her. There is a world of difference between these two approaches. Good preparation will gain you support from a sponsor.

Networking scripts like this one are designed to get you that next meeting. Once you have the green light on this informational meeting, prepare your script for that encounter. Here are some "don'ts" to avoid when you're pitching yourself.

Tired Pitch Phrases to Avoid

The following five expressions will not impress.

#1: I WANT TO PICK YOUR BRAIN

This is a gross expression. But beyond that, it can seem like you don't have a clear purpose. "I want to pick your brain" essentially says, "I hope you have some insights that I don't have. I'm looking for references, or jobs, or ideas, or . . . whatever, you name it."

#2: CAN I HAVE 20 MINUTES OF YOUR TIME TO CHAT?

Here is another expression to avoid if you are approaching someone for help. Anytime you ask someone for a chat, you're saying, "This isn't necessarily important, and the conversation won't necessarily have a direction." You may be using the word "chat" because you don't want to sound too pushy. But if you're asking a busy person for help—and most influential people are busy—a desire to chat likely won't go down well.

#3: YOU HAVE LOTS OF CONTACTS—CAN YOU SHARE THEM WITH ME?

When you say this to someone, it's as if you are asking them to open their address book and give you all the names in it. People are generally cautious about giving you more than a few names. Their contacts are precious and well earned over time. They will want to know that if they give you a name, you will follow up with that individual and do so with discretion. Asking for "lots" of contacts makes it sound like you will not treat them with care. Instead, say exactly who you'd like to talk to—for example, an executive in a particular retail chain or the head of HR for a financial institution or someone who works for a specific company. Choose a name or title that will get you inside the firm you are interested in.

#4: I NEED YOUR HELP GETTING A JOB

This phrase tests poorly because it's far too vague. It's also not great because the word "need" tends to suggest that you are without resources—not a great look when you're job searching. Even though you may need a job or a reference, there are better ways to state that. For example, "I would appreciate your help" or "I would love to have a reference from you." Positive language makes a huge difference in the way people perceive you.

#5: I'VE SENT OUT TONS OF LETTERS AND NO ONE REPLIES

This expression, along with others like "I can't seem to get that next career move" or "It's been tough slogging," gives people the idea that you are failing at a goal you have. Why do that? Never bad-mouth yourself. Instead, be very precise about your goals and the steps you have taken. Emphasize the positive, and even though you may have had a tough time getting interviews, don't let on that this has been your trajectory. People want to associate themselves with winners, so show that you're on the road to winning that next position.

All these expressions make you sound unfocused, needy, and

insecure. That is not a good start for any relationship, particularly when you're trying to impress.

Structuring Your Networking Script

What you need for any networking conversation—whether you're pitching yourself in person, virtually, by phone, or by email—is a strong, confident script that provides a compelling narrative about you. You've got only one chance to make a first impression, so create a dynamic script that inspires your contact. You can do this by following the four-step process defined by the HIRE template. And remember to use this whether you're going for an internal move or an external one.

Here's how to design your networking script.

Step 1: Create a warm and inviting opening hook that reaches out to the person you'll be talking to. Don't apologize with "I hate to bother you, but . . ."

Here are some excellent opening hooks:

- Thanks for seeing me. I appreciate your time.
- You're just the person I want to talk to about a job opportunity.
- I really value your opinion and have something I'd like to discuss with you.
- We met recently at the XYZ conference, and I'd love a few minutes of your time.
- Bill Jenkins suggested I call you about a job I'm looking into.

These openers set a good tone for your request.

Step 2: Inspire. To inspire, have a message that moves your audience to believe in you and want to help you. These are examples:

- (To a recruiter) I've heard about a job opportunity in your company, and I'd love to be considered for it since it dovetails perfectly with my background.

- (To a college friend) I'm searching for my next position in advertising, and I'm sure you'd have insight into opportunities.

- (To an executive in your company) I'd appreciate your wisdom on how I might move my career forward in this company—you are so well positioned to give me insight.

Notice that inspiration comes from showing how much you value the person you're approaching and how ready you are for a new role.

Step 3: Reinforce your message. In a meeting with your boss to discuss a new job opportunity you would like to pursue, reinforce your argument by explaining the reasons why you feel ready for this next step in your career. If your pitch is for a meeting with an HR professional, you may want to use the situation/response structure. First, describe your present situation (e.g., you're ready for a change), and then the response (you're keenly interested in the advertised job, which is perfect for you).

If you are talking to a senior leader in an industry, and your message is that you'd like to work in that sector, back up that statement with the reasons you believe this is a great next step for you—and your potential employer. For example:

1. I've become increasingly interested in this industry.

2. I believe my background positions me for such an assignment.

3. My leadership skills would be an asset.

Step 4: Engage. This is your call to action—asking for follow-through. Be as specific as possible. If you are requesting a meeting, ask, "When would be a good day to meet?" If you've met with someone, your call to action might be one of these:

- (To an industry contact) I appreciate your giving me the names of these two contacts, and I will follow up with them and keep you posted.

- (To an executive in the company you are working for) Would you be willing to pass my resume on to the head of department XYZ? Coming from you, that would really give me an advantage.

This four-step scripting process will position you as a confident, focused candidate who deserves the help you are seeking. Preparation of these clearly structured talking points means you'll be able to use them in a variety of ways.

The Networking Dialogue

The script you've prepared is only one side of a conversation. You'll want to listen carefully, ask questions, and create a fluid interaction. Here's how one job applicant successfully integrates her script into the conversation with a financial executive at a meet-and-greet.

Hook—with a grabber
Nice to meet you, Mr. Ardrossan. I have admired your leadership and know you and your bank are a champion of women.

Thank you. We've worked hard to be at the forefront of diversity and inclusion.

[a few more minutes of chitchat]

Inspire—with your message
I work for Euro Bank, heading their foreign exchange services, and I wonder if you'd have a place in your organization for someone like me.

Tell me more about yourself.

Reinforce—with proof points
1. While I enjoy my job at Euro Bank, I know that your bank has much more extensive operations—and I could see myself working in your treasury department on your foreign exchange desk or any related area.

2. During my seven years at Euro Bank, I have increased foreign exchange operations by a factor of 10 and doubled profitability.

3. I also believe I've distinguished myself as a leader overseeing a team of 12.

Very interesting! We're always looking for talent. Who do you report to at Euro Bank?

The head of trading, Eneo Jenkins.

Oh! I know him.

I've learned a great deal from him. And I should mention he's not aware of my interest in your organization.

Engage—with a call to action

I understand and will keep this confidential but would like your resume.

Of course. I'll send it to you. May I call your assistant and arrange for an appointment to continue this discussion?

Give me a few weeks, we can meet then.

I look forward to that. It has been a pleasure.

In this conversation, the job seeker had a clear goal: to get a job in that executive's organization. It never hurts—and will help you—to approach people who might see your talent and act upon it. Notice that she stayed strong, clarified what she wanted, and in the end, took control by suggesting she would make an appointment.

Be sure to follow through on any networking action that was discussed. Check that your contact has done what was promised. If not, remind that person of what was promised and your keen interest in taking next steps. Networking is an art, not a science. But the guidelines set down in this chapter should make all the difference. Expand your network. Be sure your script has the components discussed in this chapter—then deliver it well, follow up with a thank-you note, and make sure what was committed to is done. Persist, and you'll find that networking proves to be the path to success.

• • •

I've been talking about conversational scripts that can launch your job search successfully—whether they take place in an elevator, on the phone, or at a networking event. The next chapter focuses on internal conversations because firms are increasingly receptive to helping employees move ahead in their organizations. They want to hold on to strong performers like you. Your very best opportunities may well lie internally. If you want to rise in your firm, read on.

CHAPTER 8

Pitching Yourself Inside Your Company

IN TODAY'S TURBULENT JOB MARKET, more employees than ever have their eye on the exit door. That restlessness is true for all generations, but particularly for millennials. According to a Gallup poll, half of millennials don't expect to be at their current company in one year.[1] Forty-three percent of employees say they don't see opportunities for internal mobility, according to a 2021 report.[2]

But your dream job just might be waiting for you in your present company. There are many opportunities for advancement or lateral moves. According to Universum's 2022 report on the World's Most Attractive Employers, "Companies are investing heavily in reskilling existing talent and promoting people from within."[3]

It's a win-win. So ask yourself, "Would I like to stay with this company, and is there a job I'd like to do?" While the grass and dollars may look greener on the other side of the job fence, those who like their present company (and polls show many do) should consider advancing their career while staying with their current employer. It's definitely worth your while to have that conversation.

Emily He, a chief marketing officer at Microsoft, told me: "The global pandemic has given companies new priorities, and this has opened the door to new opportunities for employees and lessened the need for job-hopping."[4] This chapter will show you how to seize such opportunities by approaching the right people and creating a strong script for that next job—within your present company.

Building Your In-House Network

The first and crucial step in getting promoted within your firm is building a network of people who can help you. "Networking is a huge factor in finding new opportunities within your company," Emily He explained. "It's really about getting to know your colleagues, both within your teams but also across other departments. As you build connections with people you don't traditionally work with day-to-day, more opportunities—many you never even thought of—will arise."

Many companies have tools that help with this networking. Oracle's cloud-based Connections is one example. If your company has such a platform, use it to find the positions and people that will lead to your next opportunity. Other firms have networking groups. The Hartford Financial Services Group, for example, has internal networking programs designed to bring like-minded people together for career advancement. One of their programs is "Explore for Leadership," with a mandate "to enable individuals to explore different types of leadership career paths and determine what might be right for them."[5] Most companies have similar networking groups, and they can assist you in advancing in your current firm.

In addition to joining networking groups, seek out individuals who can help you advance. Who are the best people to speak with?

Begin with your boss. To move up in your organization, this relationship is key. It's true that many people wish to leave their jobs because of bad bosses. But if things are good—and you are seeking a career move—your boss can be your strongest advocate. Meet with that person and pitch yourself for a promotion or ask for their support in finding a job elsewhere in the company.

This can be a delicate conversation. If you've made an impressive contribution, you undoubtedly will be valued in that department. Many bosses will respect your drive and applaud your desire to stay within the firm. Tell your boss how much you have learned from her and what a positive experience it has been working under her leadership. And don't be discouraged if you raise this goal and your boss isn't immediately receptive. It may be something she has never thought of, and it's your job to show her that you are ready.

I knew someone who went to her boss and asked for a promotion, only to be told she wasn't ready for it. Her manager said: "You don't have the leadership skills for a next-level job." The job seeker's response: "Then give me a leadership role so I can prove I have what it takes." Don't let your boss discourage you. Stay with your goal!

While your manager is a key figure in your campaign for a

promotion, many other leaders can help. These include hiring managers, sponsors, and mentors.

Hiring managers can advance your career by hiring you or telling you what skills you need to develop for the job you want. Stacey Wollman, a senior sales underwriter at The Hartford, applied for an internal job that she wanted but was not quite ready for. Eighty percent of the job was dealing with workers' compensation cases. The hiring manager, the claims account director, was kind enough to follow up with her and suggest how she could find the mentoring in that area that she needed. He advised her to shadow a claims manager who handled such cases, take an online course offered by the company, and apply for the next job in that area. Hiring managers can be a huge help.

In fact, you don't have to wait until the interview to benefit from their sage advice. Wollman advises job seekers to "approach the hiring manager once you see the job posting. Explain how much you'd like to work in that department, how much the job interests you, and what background you have in that area. Say, 'I saw this position being advertised. I'd love to be considered for it and work on your team.' That way you create an early bond."[6]

A sponsor is someone who has your back and will bring your name forward when there is an internal job opportunity. The best way to find a sponsor is to identify an influential senior person who respects you and your work. For example, if your next ideal position is PR manager, you might talk to the head of that department or someone—say in HR—with whom you might have worked on a project and who liked your contribution. Once you identify the right person, ask if they'll keep their eyes open for a suitable promotion. It takes courage to reach out to these individuals, but it's an extraordinarily effective way to get ahead. Leaders are usually open to such requests if you have the credentials.

A mentor will also go to bat for you. Chris Kowalewski, chief growth officer of Compass Group, remarked to me, "You need to develop mentors on the way to building your career." He adds, "When you approach a mentor, have a clear goal in mind. Say 'I want to become a better communicator,' or 'I'm trying to get to the next level and want to understand those roles.' Pick someone you've had contact with and show you value them by being respectful and punctual in your meetings."[7]

Spend time building other relationships too. If you admire a certain executive, set up a meeting and offer to assist with a project. One person I spoke to volunteered to prepare a PowerPoint presentation for a senior person whom he wanted to get to know. This involved a briefing and a closer connection with that executive. Kowalewski says: "My style has always been that anyone in the organization has access to me. Call me, text me, whatever. I am not going to question why someone at any level is reaching out to me. I'm here to help, to fill the gaps, to make it easier for everyone else." Let this senior leader know that you'd be pleased to contribute to his organization.

To get noticed as a go-getter in your company, look for ways to assist with or lead initiatives that will raise your profile and bring you company-wide attention. This can be a charitable event or a business project. Whatever the focus, if you can add value and have the company see you as a star performer, go for it. Seek opportunities to raise your profile. Then, when you have your eye on an opportunity—or when one comes your way—you'll be ready.

Creating Your Internal Script

Once you've developed a network of senior-level influencers, get ready to meet with and ask those individuals for assistance. Here are scripts for pitching your boss, your sponsor or mentor, and a senior hiring manager.

PITCHING YOUR BOSS

You've just seen on a job board an ad for a more senior position in your department. It pays $20,000 more than you're making. As you contemplate your next move, you see passing in the hallway the very person you've decided to talk to—your boss.

You say casually, "Hey, Mike, I see there's a new position in our department: senior manager, digital services. I'm going to apply for it. I think my background is perfect for that role, and I'm wondering if I have your support?"

Your boss doesn't reply (as you might have wished) with "Sure, you're great, you have my support." Instead, he says, "You think you're ready for that role? Tell me why." For a moment, your mind goes blank, and your tongue feels twisted. But you've thought about it in advance, and you recover and pitch yourself as a strong candidate for that role. You impress your boss, and he says, "Sure, I'm in. Go for it."

This story—which really happened—required mental agility on the part of the 30-something associate. Not everyone would have the presence to make their case on the spot. Many people in that situation might "um" and "ah." My advice is never to express your interest in moving ahead without having prepared a script.

It's better to book a meeting with your manager and say

you'd like to discuss "something that's been on my mind" or "something important." Don't get into the details in an email or Zoom request. Before the meeting, make sure you've thought through what you want to say. I know a woman who, at the end of a performance review, casually mentioned that she was ready for a new position—within the department but at a higher level. Her boss said, "OK, why?" She couldn't pull her thoughts together, so he dismissed her and told her to come back when she'd figured it out. Preparation is everything.

Here's a sample script to use or modify when pitching your boss for an upgrade.

Hook—your verbal handshake
Thanks for seeing me. I appreciate your time. (or) There is something I'd like to discuss with you, and I felt it important to be face-to-face with this discussion—it's that important.

Inspire—with your message
I've been in this job for five years, I've performed at a high level, and am ready to take on a role where I can have an even greater impact.

Reinforce—with supporting points

1. I've built strong and enduring customer relationships.

2. My team has supported our customers with new and expanded services—and high levels of satisfaction.

3. I'm well versed in our company's digital initiatives and have used many of them to drive sales growth.

Engage—your call to action
I believe the digital senior manager role in our department would build on my strengths and track record.
I'd be pleased if you would support my application
for that role.

This script represents the bones of a discussion—it may
be delivered all at once as the boss listens or with intermit-
tent comments by the boss. But having such a narrative in
your mind will be invaluable in enabling you to structure the
conversation around your goals. And, in taking the initiative
and speaking with clarity and confidence, you'll show yourself as a worthy candidate who deserves serious consideration.
So, prepare.

Are there other things to keep in mind? Absolutely. You'll
want to maintain your positive tone and your optimism about
reaching your goals, and not back down if your boss is not supportive. I know one director-level banker who went to her boss
and told him she'd been offered a more senior role in another
department. But after her boss replied, "Oh, don't take that, I
need you here," she backed down and said she'd stay. Ten years
later, she is still with him, in the same role.

PITCHING A SPONSOR OR MENTOR

You also need to prepare a strong script for when you approach
a mentor or sponsor for support. Let's say, for example, that a
regional manager position has become available in your firm,
and it would be two steps above where you are now. The decision
will be made by an executive committee, and you have a close
relationship with a member of that committee. Set up a meeting

and prepare what you'll say. Here's a compelling script to deliver to your sponsor.

Hook—reach out with a grabber

I heard that there may be an opening for a new regional manager in the Caribbean, and I am interested in putting my name forward. I'd appreciate your help.

Inspire—with a message

I know I'd be a great fit for that position, and I'm ready for an international assignment.

Reinforce—with proof points

1. I have had responsibility for a smaller region and have shown I can build business within a region. Our numbers have doubled since I became head of this group.

2. My team has done really well under my leadership—they are highly motivated and work well with clients across our region.

3. I have emphasized inclusive values that have been important in creating trust between our group and our regional customers.

Engage—with a call to action

I am ready to take on the challenge, and I know the executive committee would value your opinion about me. I would love your endorsement.

Occasionally, a sponsor or mentor may come to you and say they have the perfect position for you. For example: "I am looking for a manager to handle our social media communications.

I think you would be the perfect fit—how about it?" This is like manna from heaven. Pray that such a blessing comes to you. When it does, say, "Yes, of course. Thank you, I'm good with this." Don't reply, "Me? I don't think I have the background to fill that role, I've only been with the company for a year." Even if you don't feel 100 percent qualified, you can learn on the job. If someone believes you can do the job, go for it!

PITCHING A HIRING MANAGER

Suppose you discover on your company's job board that a financial analyst position is open in another department. You're in sales but have a financial background and are keen to apply. Find a way to contact the hiring manager, through a recommendation from your boss, HR, or by directly mailing that individual. Prepare a script for that interview. Here's one:

Hook—your verbal handshake
Thank you for seeing me. I'm Emily Kim and would like to apply for your financial analyst position.

Inspire—with a message
I'm a team leader in sales but have a strong financial background from my MBA and believe I'd be an excellent fit for your financial analyst role.

Reinforce—with proof points
1. I've been working in sales for four years, the last two as team leader—so I know this company and its products well.

2. In my MBA program, I focused on financial planning, including coauthoring a prize-winning essay, "Can Anyone Tell What Your Investments Will Be Worth in Six Years or Six Months?"

3. I've been impressed by the work your department does, particularly in integrating our new acquisitions, and would be excited to join the team.

Engage—with a call to action
Will you consider me for this position?

This is a strong pitch that will energize the conversation between the candidate and the hiring manager. If you're wondering why it ends on a question, the answer is that it's best to leave the last word for the person who makes the decision. The question calls on the hiring manager to give an answer. If the answer is, "We'll see," then you say, "What can I do to put my name in the running?" Keep moving the discussion toward a result—it is a call to action.

Follow up each of these interactions with a thank-you note. Wait a week or so, and then send a query about next steps. Pursue this dialogue until you nail the job. Don't worry about being a pest or appearing too needy. You will come across as more confident if you follow up and make this hiring a top-of-mind priority for the manager.

Whatever form your initial conversations take, make sure you don't treat them casually. Your informal pitches—both those for external roles and those you deliver in quest of an internal promotion—are critical to your success as a job seeker. They may seem informal, but they are important and deserve to be well prepared.

PART III

WRITTEN SCRIPTS

So far, we've been looking at crafting and delivering conversational scripts that will set you off on your job journey with flying colors. But you'll also have to tell your story in written documents, specifically in your resume, cover letter, and thank-you notes. Part III will show you how to create standout documents that communicate your strengths, your readiness for the role, and your enthusiasm for the position. You'll learn to prepare written communications that inspire recruiters and hiring managers and move you forward in your journey.

CHAPTER 9

A Winning Resume

THE RESUME REMAINS THE GO-TO document for job seekers.

In Monster's 2022 *Future of Work* report, the resume is ranked by US recruiters as the best way hiring companies can find candidates when using online job boards.[1] And employers rank it second only to in-person interviews for assessing whether a candidate is an ideal fit. Your resume plays a major role in your success, and because it is such an important chapter in your story, it needs to be well crafted.

Contrary to popular belief, those who read resumes do give them more than a passing glance, spending an average of three to six minutes on each.[2] These readers are looking for your story—your narrative. For that reason, there must be a thread running through your resume that moves the reader to believe in you, to choose you as a candidate worthy of an interview—and a job. Hiring professionals say they value substance over style when reading resumes.[3] Think of your resume in terms of the substance it conveys.

Much of the literature on resume construction, however, focuses on design, format, fonts, colors, key words, and length, as well as on the role of the Applicant Tracking System (ATS). To be sure, these tips are useful. It's important to avoid overly stylized typefaces and stick to traditional ones like Arial, Calibri, Georgia, Helvetica, and Times New Roman. Candidates should not use columns or insert tables. The ATS evaluation (discussed later in this chapter) also must be kept in mind.

But those tips ignore a critical dimension: the deeper structure of your resume. This is the set of interlocking arguments that tell your story and persuade the reader that you are an ideal candidate. To truly make your case, you need a "resume script." This is the narrative that uses the HIRE template featured in this book and shows you as a standout candidate. This chapter explains how to design such a resume.

Be Sure There's a Good Fit

Before drafting your resume, make sure you are a suitable candidate for the job. According to one study, employers find that about 75 percent of those applying for a position are not qualified for the job.[4] They lack the skills and background and are quickly rejected by a computer algorithm or person reading the application. Don't apply for every job in sight—only those you're best suited for.

Even when a company reaches out to you, think twice before responding. Every month, millions of companies post millions of jobs on LinkedIn pages. Along with LinkedIn, companies use sites such as Monster, ZipRecruiter, and Indeed, as well as their own job portals, to track down promising candidates. Still, the postings that turn up on your LinkedIn pages and these portals may be far removed from your interests and skills. Be selective and put your energy into the positions that fully align with your qualifications.

Creating Your Resume Script

Once you decide to apply for a position, your resume will provide the key to opening doors that lie ahead. To craft that winning resume, use the HIRE template. It will allow you to offer employers a strong, persuasive narrative about you and your qualifications. To create a winning resume, follow these steps.

STEP 1: CRAFT CONTACT INFORMATION TO GRAB YOUR READER

Your contact information is the first thing a recruiter will look at. It's the H or "hook" in HIRE. Make it strong and clear. Include your first and last name, phone number (personal, not work), email, LinkedIn address, and a link to your website or professional portfolio if you have one. This aspect of your script should be strong, with your name centered in bold letters, in a font size that's 18–24 points. Your contact information should be in a 10–12 size font. This is your verbal handshake, so make it appealing.

STEP 2: CREATE AN INSPIRING SUMMARY STATEMENT

The summary statement comes next. It's your opportunity to inspire (it's the I in HIRE). Make sure this message is clear and forceful. Ask yourself, "What's the one compelling idea I want to get across about myself?"

Ideally, it is *one sentence and only one sentence*. A single sentence provides a unifying format. If you have too many sentences or a run-on sentence (which is like having multiple sentences), you'll have no unity. That creates a blurred vision of you. I've seen resumes that have summary statements that are four or five sentences long. That becomes a jumble of ideas and an unfocused picture of the candidate.

Your summary statement must be specific. This rules out generic descriptions filled with buzzwords like this: "An enthusiastic, motivated, and highly results-driven professional, offering over 12 years' experience in successive positions with several companies, with the ability to liaise with internal/external departments, focused on demonstrating exceptional customer service, getting the job done and consistently meeting and exceeding company goals." Every buzzword has been stuffed into that long sentence. But what does it really say? Do we know anything about this person? This could be an executive, a manager, or a specialist in any industry. It could be someone in high tech or in sales. It could be someone with talent—or not. It's anyone's guess. In fact, the individual featured in this resume is a restaurant cook.

Let's say you're responding to an ad for a cybersecurity senior engineer position. A well-targeted summary statement would be: "Senior-level manager with 15 years' experience overseeing information security in two financial firms." A still better statement would indicate not only what the job seeker did, but what she or he achieved. The improved version: "A senior-level cyber security manager who put in place much admired, industry-standard programs that fully protected two financial firms from ransomware and other malicious attacks."

Make sure your summary statement is a message, not a career objective. Some job seekers open with "Objective: Seeking an entry-level position in the financial industry that would use my interpersonal skills." One such summary statement I came across was this: "Committed to building my career in the retail industry in an organization that has a strong culture, flexible working environment, and excellent opportunities for me to use my talents and support the company, the industry, and society."

That's a career goal, not a message about the strengths this candidate would bring to a future employer. This generic objective statement betrays a lack of interest in the specific job advertised. I would never hire a candidate who wrote such a statement. I did once receive such a generic objective statement from a job applicant: "To use my writing skills, research experience, strategic thinking, and creativity in an advertising, marketing or communications role." The scope of this objective statement showed that the candidate wasn't particularly interested in the role advertised in my leadership communications company. We didn't interview her.

Your summary statement should use strong, clear language that inspires. Choose active verbs rather than nouns. Don't say you were a leader; say you *led*. Choose verbs like *built, earned, exceeded, delivered, won, produced, increased, surpassed,* and *transformed*. These will make your summary more compelling.

Given these requirements we've discussed, what does an ideal summary statement or message look like? Here are three excellent ones:

1. A seasoned HR professional who has led teams of high achievers in designing and building programs that reached over 50,000 employees and exceeded targets in two successive retail industry organizations.

2. An energetic art director who, during a 10-year career in two acclaimed firms, has produced five award-winning campaigns earning agency clients national profile and increased market share.

3. An experienced executive with a strong track record in managing, building, and leading a major $30 billion global commercial real estate firm in a series of increasingly senior positions.

Note the clarity of these statements. Keep your summary sentence simple and well structured. Don't try to pack too much into that one statement. It is the most important single sentence in the resume, and it needs to be an inspiring message.

STEP 3: REINFORCE YOUR MESSAGE WITH A SET OF SUPPORTING POINTS

The reinforcing points are the "R" in HIRE. They should line up with and support your summary statement. Those points will be in your "Professional Experience" section. If you've had a long career, this section will take up the better part of two pages. For a shorter career, this section will be less than one page.

Build this career section by listing the companies you've worked for and their locations, in reverse chronological order. Under each company put the job titles you've held in that organization, and the years you held them. Provide a one-sentence message for each job just below the job title. Think of that statement as a message that makes clear your contribution in each role. Make sure it aligns with your summary statement.

For example, the HR professional whose summary statement was mentioned earlier might have this message for her most recent (and current) job: "I lead a team of 5 HR managers and 20 HR professionals who have collectively contributed new programs, bold initiatives, and bottom-line results for our company."

The second candidate might have this message for his current job: "In this role, I have led a team of art directors and freelancers to develop and deliver award-winning campaigns for highly satisfied client companies."

The third candidate might state: "As president of the firm's commercial leasing organization, I oversee a $16 billion business in six countries with profit and loss responsibility and over 12,000 employees."

In creating those statements for each job you've held, you will be reinforcing your summary statement with a set of chronologically arranged points that align with and advance your main message.

STEP 4: CREATE A SET OF BULLET POINTS UNDER EACH JOB STATEMENT

Reinforce each of those job sentences with a set of bulleted points. For recent positions, you can have more bullets than for earlier positions. Anywhere from two to four bullets is a good rule of thumb. The bullets give hard facts about what you've accomplished. Use dollar amounts, percentage increases, number of people reached, and bottom-line results.

The HR professional in the preceding example might have the following bullets for her current job:

- Developed a plan that provided childcare support to more than 50 employees.

- Introduced a company-wide mental health plan that is heavily subscribed.
- Championed a highly successful "Productivity Matters" program for executives.

The creative designer in the example might support his current job message with the following bullet points:

- Hired two creatives, one copywriter, and a filmmaker.
- Provided creative direction for two campaigns.
- Won a Webby as well as accolades from clients.

The president of the real estate division might have these bullets under the current job:

- Built the division from $10 billion to $16 billion.
- Grew profitability by 20 percent.
- Restructured to create a geographical leadership team.

The bullets should all start with a verb or action word, as these bullets do. Avoid bulleted statements that do not start with the same type of word, as in the following:

- Analyze product package, fabrics, trims, and accessories.
- Helping with order confirmation.
- Closely monitors choice of fabrics.
- When needed, follow-up testing material of fabrics and garments.

Your bulleted items should also be as specific as possible about the impact of the programs you've developed or overseen. Eighty-five percent of recruiters say it's important to provide metrics that illustrate your accomplishments.[5] The bullets present quantifiable results, either explaining numbers of people reached or the financial impact of the programs. As Nagaraj Nadendla, senior vice president of product development at Oracle, remarked in an interview with me: "The prospective employee should give enough reasons for the employer to take a chance with them."[6] The bullet points provide concrete reasons why the recruiter can believe in the job candidate.

STEP 5: ADD OTHER SECTIONS

In finishing your resume, you'll want some short sections:

In an "Education" section, be precise about the names of your colleges or universities, including their location (University of California, Irvine) and the degrees you earned, fully spelled out (Bachelor of Science in Chemistry, not BS in Chemistry). Put the most recent degree on top, and include any additional courses you've taken.

A "Certificates" section will show you have won awards or gained certification either professionally or personally. For example, you may wish to post that you've taken a business course like those posted on Coursera. Or indicate that you've taken a program in public speaking, musical certification, or climate leadership. Even sports awards or accomplishments can be included. If you're a black belt in karate or have attained a similar level in another sport or hobby, say so.

A "Skills" section will highlight specific skills not mentioned in your career section. This would include, for example, software design, programming, and language skills.

STEP 6: MAKE SURE YOU HAVE THE IMPORTANT KEY WORDS

For many jobs, the first cut is made by a computer that scans your resume. According to a ResumeLab study, more than 95 percent of Fortune 500 companies use Applicant Tracking System (ATS) software to streamline the review of submissions.[7] But here's the catch: many companies do not use the ATS for senior appointments or specialized roles. One recruiter told me that even though her firm, a large financial institution, has ATS software, it is not used to screen the majority of resumes for senior-level or specialized positions. That's because she has information given to her by the hiring manager that allows her to differentiate a winning candidate from someone who may have the right on-paper credentials, but not be as good a fit. As she put it, "We have knowledge that the robot doesn't have."

Nevertheless, if a job posting attracts a large number of applicants—say 400 or more—it is typically difficult for a firm to avoid using ATS screening. Think positively about this computer vetting and recognize that it reinforces good resume practices. The ATS scan examines your educational background, the companies you worked for, and how long you were with each one. Make sure that information is clear. It also looks for key words to make sure the fit is a good one. If you can pick up some of the language of the job posting—without overdoing such repetition—you'll help yourself.

Chris Rodgers, CEO of Colorado SEO Pros, says: "This system is looking for words that relate to specific skill sets in the jobs being advertised. For example, in a junior finance position, an employer might list a specific finance software that it wants a candidate to be well-versed in." He goes on to say, "If you see this software required in the jobs you're applying for, that's a clue this is a key word you should work into your resume." And don't mention it just once. Rodgers explains: "That key word should appear in the top of your resume as part of your profile, as well as in the body of your resume."[8]

The ATS is very literal in what it's looking for, so don't try to be creative or use acronyms. If you put down that you have an MBA, or are a CFA, the machine won't necessarily recognize these credentials unless you spell out these abbreviations.[9]

Finally, clear writing is all-important to the machine. "The robot wants you to be clear and to the point," explains Nagaraj Nadendla, vice president at Oracle and responsible for Oracle Recruiting Cloud. "The reason is that it's easier for the machine to process such writing than cumbersome, jargon-filled prose. It's also true that if you plug key words into a straightforward narrative, they appear more honest than as though you stuff them awkwardly into sentences."[10]

Brett Tearney, a vice president at ServiceNow, agrees. "Machines are looking for simple, concise commentary—words the ATS recognizes so it can create a relationship between common terms," he says. "The more terms you put in, or the more flowery language you use, the more difficulty the machine will have. The machine would be impressed if you talk about your collaborative skill set, the things you've done, the steps you've taken, the accomplishments you've had. Simple and to the point is usually the better way. It also likes active verbs rather than passive verbs. Active verbs up the score of the application, as opposed to those words that are passive."[11]

STEP 7: DO A FINAL EDIT

Before you submit your resume, give it a final edit.

Begin by checking to make sure you have used the HIRE template successfully. It should: (1) Hook your reader with your personal information at the top of the resume; (2) Inspire with a strong summary statement; and (3) Reinforce with your career experience and lead statement for each job you've had, supported by bullet points that show your impact in each job. As for (4) Engage, the final component of the HIRE template, this task is accomplished by the cover letter attached to your resume. The sample resume that ends this chapter shows those first three elements (and the next chapter discusses cover letters).

In doing this final edit, check that your resume language is easy to read. As mentioned, the ATS screening wants simplicity and accuracy, as does your reader. A well-crafted resume transcends information, bloated language, and jargon. It is much more than a collection of facts or job titles, or data and descriptions. It is a set of persuasive arguments that will move the reader to believe in you and your suitability for the advertised role. To achieve this focus on your narrative, write with a clear, natural voice.

Make sure your document is carefully formatted, too, with ample margins on all sides. Some people advise limiting your resume to one page. Others—and I am one of them—suggest that those with a short to mid-length career stick to one page, while job seekers with a longer career, many accomplishments, and several employers should use two pages. Whichever you choose, don't end midway down the page. It will look like you've run out of accomplishments. Keep it to one or two full pages.

Carefully check your text for spelling mistakes, grammatical problems, and typos. Many employers will dismiss a resume with a single typo. Proper names are not picked up by spell-check, so you need to look particularly closely at them. Ask a friend or family member to proofread your resume, too. And you can forget your chances with an employer who sees her company's name misspelled.

STEP 8: INCLUDE A COVER LETTER

Once you've finalized the resume, write a cover letter to accompany it, unless the employer specifically asks that you not send one. The cover letter will enable you to create a connection with the hiring company by personalizing your message.

Resume writing is an art. It requires excellent communication skills and a narrative that tells your story clearly and persuasively. The sample resume shown next illustrates the guidelines in this chapter, albeit the font sizes are smaller to fit this book's format. Follow the directions discussed in this chapter, and you'll inspire hiring professionals with a top-notch resume and cover letter that personalizes your submission. Our next chapter will show you how to craft such a letter.

HEIDI ARDROSSAN

hardrossan@connectmail.com   c: 559-555-0110   www.linkedin.com/in/heidiardrossan/

A seasoned HR professional who has led teams of high achievers in designing and building programs that reached over 100,000 employees and exceeded targets in two successive retail industry organizations

PROFESSIONAL EXPERIENCE

Marketco, Inc.   **Phoenix, Arizona**
Senior Manager, Human Relations   **April 2017–Present**

I lead a team of 5 HR managers and 20 HR professionals who have collectively contributed new programs, bold initiatives, and bottom-line results for our company.

- Developed a plan that provided childcare support to 50+ employees
- Introduced company-wide mental health plan that is heavily subscribed
- Championed highly successful "Productivity Matters" program for executives

Willet Clothiers   **Fresno, California**
Manager, Human Relations   **Jan. 2012–March 2017**

Successfully managed programs as company grew by 30,000 employees worldwide

- Established robust communication links with European offices
- Improved employee satisfaction by 40% with our "Open Door" program
- Repeatedly recognized by management for these contributions

EDUCATION

Penn State University   **University Park, Penn.**
Bachelor of Arts, Business Administration   **December 2011**

SKILLS

- Fluent in English, Spanish, and German
- Expert in Microsoft Office, Photoshop, and Oracle Financial Training
- Diversity trainer

CHAPTER 10

A Killer Cover Letter

IT'S SAID THAT MARK TWAIN once wrote, "I didn't have time to write a short letter, so I wrote a long one instead." These words are a good reminder to job applicants. It's much better to write a short, well-crafted letter than a long one. Recruiters and hiring managers are busy people! They are less likely to read long letters than short ones. I learned about keeping letters short early in my career when my responsibilities included writing letters for the CEO of a major North American bank. His letters had to be a single page—typically three short paragraphs. They also had to be gracious, clear, compelling, and well structured. You'll want to create cover letters that fulfill these requirements. Those letters will be a huge asset in your job hunt.

Why Write a Cover Letter?

Not every employer requests a letter, but always include one when it is asked for, and even when it is not. Why? The simple, compelling reason is that including a cover letter allows you to say a lot about yourself—who you are, what kind of personality you have, and why you are excited about the job opportunity. And it allows a more personal tone than the resume.

This full disclosure is what hiring professionals look for and love. A 2022 ResumeLab survey of 200 hiring managers and recruiters found that 83 percent of respondents said cover letters are important in deciding which candidates to hire.[1] A poll by the recruitment firm Robert Half similarly notes that 90 percent of executives consider cover letters "invaluable when assessing candidates."[2] And in still another study, recruiters say they find these letters "can provide valuable insight." This same study shows that candidates who submitted customized cover letters received over 50 percent more interviews than those who didn't.[3] Those numbers say a lot about why you should take time to write a well-crafted letter.

You may wonder, "Will my letter be read by a real person?" In fact, more letters are read than you might think. One editorial staff member at The Muse found that recruiters and hiring managers said they review a wide variety of cover letters, including those of all qualified candidates, those of candidates being considered for the next step in the hiring process, and even those of borderline candidates.[4] This is a wide swathe of applicants. If you have the credentials or come close, your letter will be read.

Should you submit a cover letter when one is not required? In most cases, yes. In the ResumeLab study, a full 77 percent of recruiters said they'd give preference to candidates who send a cover letter, *even when these letters are optional*.[5] If you're applying for a technical job, you may not need one, but it never hurts. And for a leadership position or one that requires soft skills, it's a good idea to include one. The only time you should not submit a cover letter is when the hiring firm says not to or when you're applying online and there is no way to upload a letter.

A well-written cover letter strengthens your case in several ways. To begin with, it shows you hold the company in high esteem—a welcome note for those doing the hiring. Do your research and use phrases such as "I have long admired your firm," or "Your mission is a powerful one," or "I have always wanted to work for your company." And be specific. A winning cover letter must be carefully customized. If you say, "I've long admired your firm," show something concrete that you admire. Its vision? Its products? Its culture? Its leadership? You might note you've been inspired by the CEO's podcasts. If you've ever met any senior person in that company, you can also say you were struck by her vision or passion. Even if you're applying for a position inside your present company, a cover letter can show your enthusiasm for that employer and the reasons you want to stay with the firm.

The cover letter also allows you to show how your experience and skills make you an excellent fit for the advertised role. No resume can do that as warmly as a letter can. Make clear that the description of your skills and experience aligns with the job profile. You can use the language of the job description, but don't do so in such a way that you sound like you're simply parroting the ad. This letter should be in your own voice.

A cover letter can also explain career gaps or situations where a job proved a poor fit for your talents. For example, you might say, "I've had many different types of jobs, but they all show my broad passion for marketing." A letter can create a unified picture of you, one that closes any gaps and smooths out the rough edges in your work history.

Finally, the letter conveys your confidence and professionalism. To strike the right tone, select language that is bold but not cocky. Say "I believe that," "I am confident that," "I would appreciate a meeting with you," and "should you choose me, I will deliver."

Four Qualities of a Winning Cover Letter

Here are four qualities that every cover letter should have.

First, it should show your passion for your work—and for the advertised position. It's tough to convey enthusiasm in a resume. You can hardly say, "I loved my second job," or "my third one was awesome." This tone would likely fall on deaf ears. But in your cover letter you can come alive and show your excitement about the positions you've held and the role you're applying for.

My son Ben Egnal told me that when he writes a cover letter, the heart of it reads something like this: "I am an enthusiastic art director and am hungry to create award-winning campaigns—and I believe your agency would provide the perfect environment to do the best work of my career." This is bold, enthusiastic language that positions him and the agency he wishes to join as high achieving. That passion is contagious. Every employer wants to hire people with strong commitment and high energy.

Separate yourself from the pack of job seekers by inspiring your reader with language that reaches for the stars. Include words like *love, excited, enthusiastic, committed,* and *believe.*

Second, your letter must be customized. According to the ResumeGo study,[6] a generic letter is not much better than no letter at all. Only 12.5 percent of generic letters receive a callback (compared with 10.7 percent of callbacks for resumes submitted with no letter). When you write, carefully target the letter for that job and company.

Third, your letter should use natural, conversational language—and be free from jargon. No one will be impressed if you state that you can "optimize marketing outreach" or "interface with end-users." Eliminate complicated word patterns like "I have an ability to deploy state-of-the-art solutions" or "I can prospect new business opportunities and strategize communication initiatives." Junk the jargon and speak clearly and in your natural voice. Be real. Be authentic. Be sincere.

Fourth, your letter should be flawless. Read it over closely and get someone else to do so as well. "People make mistakes in specifics," says Marissa Dyck, who is director of people and operations and interviews candidates for The Humphrey Group. "Someone applied for the advertised position in 'The Humphreys Group,' misspelling the name of our company." That's a good way to have your application summarily dismissed. I've heard of cases where applicants get the name of the job wrong, perhaps because they're sending a generic letter to all the firms they're approaching.

Keep in mind that spellcheck does not deal with proper nouns. If you're relying on it to catch your mistakes, you'll be let down. Getting the specifics correct shows you are careful with details, you care enough to get things right, and you will deliver polished and accurate work if you are hired.

Scripting Your Cover Letter with the HIRE Template

To create a winning cover letter, structure it with the HIRE template.

Start off with the salutation (Dear Ms. Harum . . .). The salutation opens your letter—it's a doorway to all that follows. Be respectful and specific. Never write, "To Whom It May Concern" or use a generic title like "Vice President, Sales." Do your research and find the name of the appropriate person. If you can't find the exact person, select the individual who is most likely to review your application.

Marissa Dyck explains: "It stands out to me when someone has taken the time to figure out who might be reading the application." Avoid overly casual salutations like "Hi Jeanette" or "Hey Vincent." This is not a time to get chummy. On the other hand, avoid any salutation that sounds abrupt, like "Adeola" or "Bill." The best salutation is "Dear Ms. Reynolds" or "Good morning Mr. Singh." The only time to use the person's first name ("Dear Terry") is if you have met that individual before. With the salutation in place, follow these four steps.

STEP 1: CREATE YOUR HOOK

The hook (or grabber) forms the opening sentence of your cover letter. It introduces you and shows the reader that you are enthusiastic about the job you're applying for. It makes clear you are connected in some way, personally or emotionally, to the company.

A good opener might be: "I am applying for the position of manager of data systems and am excited by the prospect of working in your company." This focus on the company is equivalent to an in-person opening like this: "I am so glad to meet you. I've heard so much about you." This is a better alternative than duller openings ("I would like to apply for the role of IT manager you have advertised on LinkedIn") and egotistical grabbers ("I'm excited to see the ad for a senior sales representative because I would fill this role perfectly"). Both dull and egotistical openings test poorly face-to-face, so don't use them in a letter.

STEP 2: INSPIRE WITH A STRONG MESSAGE

The second sentence in your first paragraph is the message. It is the most important sentence in your letter, and it should inspire by positioning you as a desirable candidate for the role.

Don't try to pack everything you've done and will do into this message statement. That leads to an overcrowded, unreadable main idea, such as: "With a multifaceted record of leadership in two dynamic environments in the field of radiation equipment manufacturing, sales, and operations, I would bring the strong credentials that would enable me to increase profitability, improve productivity, and reduce operating costs to your organization."

My first rule for your message statement (and all prose) is if you can't say it in one breath, it's too long. No recruiter wants to be hit with a blast of verbiage. In this example, it's difficult to even understand what the candidate is saying. Make your message clear, concise, and to the point. Like this: "I believe my experience in three successive IT roles would equip me to successfully lead your systems development team to new heights." Or: "My strengths as a media relations professional will provide the seasoned leadership to expand your firm's social media presence." Or: "I believe my experience in M&A law dovetails perfectly with this dynamic role." These messages convey enthusiasm about the position and make clear the strong fit between the applicant's qualifications and the job. They are simple, clear, and compelling.

STEP 3: REINFORCE YOUR MESSAGE

Once you've stated your message, proceed to the second paragraph. Provide the proof points that reinforce your message. Present these points all in one paragraph if they're short or in separate paragraphs if they are longer. They can be organized chronologically or as a set of reasons. Let's say your message is this: "My experience as a communications leader in two companies dovetails fully with the advertised role." Reinforce this message with the following two chronologically arranged proof points (each in its own paragraph):

1. Between 2015 and 2019, at Fabrico, in my position as manager of internal communications, I was responsible for executive communications, including speeches, PowerPoint presentations, videos, and town halls. During that time, my team and I contributed to Fabrico's extraordinary growth, creating a set of key messages about the company.

2. Since 2019, at TriCorp, as senior manager of communications, I have had a still broader set of responsibilities. Along with helping to design executive communication strategies, I've worked with our very diverse employee base, assisting the efforts of both the HR and PR departments. These efforts have been recognized both in the company and the industry—where TriCorp

stands out for its excellent approach to communications. Employee engagement has increased from 60 percent to 95 percent.

These proof points, and others like them, represent the body of your letter.

STEP 4: END WITH ENGAGEMENT

In the concluding paragraph of your cover letter, restate your interest in the position and outline next steps as you would like to see them. This shows how engaged you are—it's your call to action. It's important to sketch in what you would like to see happen without being presumptuous. Avoid these pitfalls:

- Don't tell the reader what they must conclude. ("As you can see, I pride myself on being an excellent team developer.") That's condescending.

- Don't imply that the hiring manager won't do her job. ("If I don't hear from you, I will contact you in a week.")

- Don't sound tentative. ("I hope you will be interested in me.") Avoid words like *hope*, *maybe*, *possibly*, and *if*.

Instead, be upbeat in your conclusion. Here's an example: "Thank you for your consideration. I look forward to the prospect of meeting you virtually or in person and discussing how I can make a strong contribution to your corporate communications department."

Close the letter with your first and last name and add your

phone number and email. When your phone rings, answer it—because it just might be the recruiter inviting you to an interview.

A Sample Cover Letter

Here is a sample letter using the HIRE template.

Dear Ms. Carruthers,

Hook—with a grabber
I am applying for the client relationship manager role in the New York City office of Holdco, a company I have long admired for its outstanding training programs.

Inspire—with your message
I believe my eight years of client-facing experience in two corporations makes me a strong candidate for this position.

Reinforce—with proof points
In my present firm, Popular Bank, I support our clients company-wide with their training needs. Various metrics during my three years at Popular Bank show the high level of satisfaction our clients have with our training. Before that, I was an intern at City Bank, where I had an amazing mentor who awakened my passion for working with clients.

Engage—with a call to action

I would love to be part of your team and thank you for your consideration. I look forward to the prospect of an interview and employment with Holdco.

Sincerely,
Vijay Kumar
647-555-0100
vkumar@yourmail.com

An effective cover letter using the techniques discussed in this chapter will make a huge difference in your likelihood of getting an interview. Cover letters enable you to tell your story, put a personal stamp on your application, and connect with the hiring firm even before they meet you. Writing cover letters should be a no-brainer when it comes to building a relationship with a prospective employer or winning a job with your current employer. Take the time to write one, customize it, and put your best self forward.

Just as a cover letter creates a personal connection when you submit your resume, sending thank-you notes deepens relationships throughout your search. Writing notes of gratitude is a must for any job seeker who wants to retain the goodwill of a hiring manager, recruiter, or anyone who has helped along the way. See the next chapter for how to write a great thank-you note.

CHAPTER 11

How to Say Thank You

A CAREER CONVERSATION SHOULDN'T END when you leave the room. You want to be in the good graces of those who assist you. Yet a LinkedIn poll showed that 40 percent of job seekers say they don't always send a note after a job interview. Failing to do so burns bridges you may want to cross again as your career continues. It's also plain, old-fashioned courtesy to send a thank-you note. If someone has given you their time or advice, they deserve to hear back from you. Showing appreciation never goes out of style.

I once met with a job candidate who sought my advice. After spending over an hour with him, reviewing his resume and cover letter and sharing contacts, I never received a "thank you." Nor did he bother to tell me that he landed a job. I heard it from a relative of his. That was disappointing, and I wouldn't help him again. Showing gratitude is an act of politeness and indicates good character. It reinforces ties with those who helped you and makes it likely that they will assist you in the future. Be sure to follow up with your thanks.

Handwritten Notes: The Gold Standard

Even if you've said "thank you" at the end of your meeting, that's not enough. That same day—even better, within a few hours—write to the person you met with and express your appreciation. And if at all possible, send a handwritten note. That's the gold standard. Such notes speak volumes.

Chris Kowalewski, chief growth officer for Compass Group, told me: "I carry a box of thank-you cards in my briefcase. When someone hears your name, what reaction do you want them to have? A handwritten thank-you note leaves a positive, lasting impression." I asked Kowalewski if an email thank-you note would be a good alternative if you don't know the person's address. He replied: "Don't send an email, don't send a text." If you don't know the person's address, ask for it at the end of the meeting. Say, "May I please have the address where you work?"[1] That may be a work-from-home address or a company address.

Still, if you can't get that address, or feel your note won't reach them the same day, an email note, sent within hours of the meeting, is a sound alternative.

Don't feel the need to send a gift with your letter. Some job seekers include a small gift or gift cards with their notes, but that is unnecessary and may create ethical issues if it is sent to a hiring manager. Stay clear of appearing to try to curry favors.

Thanking Everyone Who Helps You

Securing that next position requires help—lots of it. Be sure to show your appreciation to *everyone*. Begin by thanking anyone you network with. That includes friends who have given you leads or a colleague who provides an important introduction. It includes the executive who is a family friend and offers valuable guidance. Follow up these conversations with a note of appreciation. Thank those who help you draft your resume or cover letter. This could be a recruiter, a colleague, a coach, or a family member. Express your gratitude to them all.

I was asked by an acquaintance if I would help her son find an internship. I agreed and passed on to this young man two high-quality contacts. Shortly afterward, I heard back from one of them that she had spent an hour with him and offered him an internship in her firm. She said to him, "Let me know if you are interested." She never heard back or even received a thank-you note. This was extraordinarily embarrassing for me, and disappointing for the woman who offered him an internship. Would she bring him aboard after this response? Not at all! Would I give him any more leads? No.

Whether the conversation was virtual or in-person, thank that individual. Emphasize what you learned and how the interview excited you about the position and the company. If your future boss interviews you, convey your enthusiasm for the job and for the prospect of working on that leader's team.

If you've been vetted by members of a team, follow up with the individual who brought the group together. If you have met with a series of individuals in separate interviews, send a brief note to each of them. Customize your thank yous to reflect the specific discussions you've had. These people are more likely to put in a good word for you if you show the courtesy of thanking them.

The same thanks should be expressed once you accept a position. For example, after the hire, you will likely meet with the

HR manager to work out the details, such as salary, reporting structure, and benefits. Just because you got the job doesn't mean you stop being polite.

Even thank those who don't have openings for you. Perhaps you have written to a department head in a firm you have always wanted to work for. You hear back but find out there are no openings. Follow up with an immediate "thank you." And don't give up on that executive. If she honors you enough to say, "stay in touch," definitely follow up. Do it soon, so she doesn't forget you. Reaffirm your admiration for the company.

Finally, thank family and friends who have stood by you during this entire process. Make them feel part of your big win. You don't necessarily have to thank them with an email or hand-written letter; that might appear overly formal. But show your gratitude by taking them to dinner, sending flowers, or giving them a small token of appreciation.

Three Guidelines for a Thank-You Note

Writing thank-you notes may seem like a straightforward process. After all, you've probably written a few in the past. While it may seem easy to dash off one of these letters, be sure to get all aspects right. Good letters are part of your campaign to land that ideal job. Incorporate the following three guidelines into your thank-you notes.

FIRST, BE SPECIFIC

To begin with, the best notes are tailored. They show that you didn't just crank out a form letter. The phrase "thank you" originally meant, "I will remember what you did for me."

Your script should say what the conversation did for you. Mention specific things you learned about the person, the company, or the industry. If it was a networking meeting, you may mention that you appreciate the insights you gained about the industry. If it's a job interview you had, say you were particularly gratified to learn about the company's work-from-home protocols or its mission. You can even get more specific if the interviewer mentioned a book or a report you should read or a contact you should reach out to.

SECOND, USE WARM, EMPATHETIC LANGUAGE

Make sure to express yourself warmly; you want to sound like an actual human being. Recently, I received a thank you that resonated with warm phrases. Here are the opening lines: "It was an absolute pleasure meeting you today! Thank you for taking the time with me. I so enjoyed getting to know you, and I loved our free flow of conversation and how varied it was." Such language makes the reader feel great about the new contact. Tell the interviewer how much you enjoyed the meeting and that you look forward to being in touch.

THIRD, BENEFIT FROM THE POWER OF THE HIRE TEMPLATE

As with every other script in this book, the HIRE template allows you to make the strongest case in your thank-you notes. They should be specific and warm but should also have a message that promotes you as a strong candidate. Don't lose an opportunity to make your case. Consider this negative example: the following script is warm and gracious, but it lacks a compelling message and proof points about the candidate.

Hi [Name],

It was great to meet with you today on Zoom! Thank you for answering my questions and telling me about your experience working at Company XYZ. Judging by what you said, it seems like an awesome place to work. I especially loved hearing about your decision to join the firm.

I will stay in touch as I continue my job search. I will take your advice and contact the people you suggested I reach out to. And if you hear of any openings in your software development department, please let me know so I can apply.

All the best,
Aamir Wasti

This response nowhere makes the case for the candidate's strengths. You never want to miss an opportunity to do that.

Examples of Thank Yous that Use the HIRE Template

The examples that follow show how to unleash the power of HIRE to structure your script and show your exceptional qualities. These examples are also specific and warm.

THE CONVERSATIONAL THANK YOU

Always say thank you to the person assisting you at the end of the phone call, Zoom conversation, or interview. Just remember, the in-person appreciation you convey is *in addition to* the written note you'll send after the encounter. Here's an example of that thank you at the end of a conversation.

Suppose you've been talking to a department head in your company. When the meeting ends, look her in the eye, and deliver your hook or opener: "What a pleasure to meet with you. I really enjoyed our conversation."

Then comes your inspiring message: "I am so excited about this role, which would allow me to enhance the PR function and bring a higher profile to our executives."

In this short exchange, there's no need to reinforce the message with proof points, but engage at the end by indicating next steps: "I look forward to the prospect of meeting your VP who oversees this role. I believe I would be a good fit." Or "I'll await next steps." Notice that this script is short and positive. Its tone is just right, too: the candidate says he "would" be a good fit, not "will" be a fit. In that word choice, he shows he's confident but not presumptuous. This final sentence in the letter shows follow-through and a good call to action.

A WRITTEN THANK YOU

Your written follow-up note will be more detailed than the short conversational exchange. Here is an example of a written thank you for an executive who just interviewed you.

Hook—with a grabber
Thank you so much for the opportunity to meet with you and discuss the possibility of a position in the Treasury department.

Inspire—with your message
I was excited going into the meeting, and after hearing
you speak about your organization and the direction it's
taking, I am even more inspired now.

Reinforce—with proof points
My years of experience in foreign exchange and
domestic transactions position me well for a role in
your department.

    I also believe my collaborative skills will support your
goals of building a treasury that is well connected to the
rest of the bank.

Engage—with a call to action
It would be an honor to be part of your team, and I look
forward to next steps.

Best regards,
Juliette

Note that this letter, structured with the HIRE template,
has a good flow. It is also warm and appreciative and sells the
candidate's credentials. The reinforce section is short (only two
short points) since it would be self-centered to repeat the full
pitch. The last sentence clearly defines next steps.

THE THANK YOU AT THE END OF A JOB SEARCH

After you're hired, be sure to share the good news with all
those who assisted you all along the way. This will bolster their

confidence in you and make them want to help you again. A quick email to a colleague might read like this:

Hi Elisha,

Hook—with a grabber
Thanks again for telling me about the job that was advertised internally.

Inspire—with your message
I went for it and learned this week that I've been hired.

Reinforce—with proof points
It's a great step forward for me and gives me managerial responsibility.

Engage—with a call to action
I look forward to celebrating with you. My treat!

Vijay

A longer note is in order if someone has helped you in a more comprehensive way. I was delighted to receive the following email from someone I had supported in her search for an internship.

Good morning Judith,

Hook—with a grabber

I wanted to give you a conclusion to my internship search! I decided to accept a position at a boutique PR agency.

(Inspire—with your message

Thank you so much again for everything you've done for me.

Reinforce—with proof points

You connected me with some great people. You gave my resume an overhaul and welcomed me into your home to chat with you. I am so amazed by all the work that you've done and am so thankful that you took time out of your busy schedule to share some of your expertise.

Engage—with a call to action

I hope we can keep in touch, and I look forward to reading your book when it's finished!

Best,
Allyssa

The beauty of this last letter is that it shows gratitude for all the help the job candidate has received and personalizes the message by thanking me for welcoming her into my home. The writer also adds a nice touch when she says, "I look forward to reading your book." This is a truly elegant and gracious letter.

• • •

Showing appreciation is polite and positions you well for any future openings or for networking at a later time. Andrew Seaman, senior editor at LinkedIn, observed in an article that recruiters and hiring managers seem "genuinely touched when they hear from job seekers after conversations."[2]

Job search experts and recruiters who responded to the LinkedIn survey on the topic all agreed that sending a thank-you note is likely to improve your chances of success. Organizations value individuals with excellent interpersonal skills. Showing appreciation demonstrates that ability. A prompt, warm thank you strengthens ties with those who helped you. And if a hiring manager is on the fence about a candidate, a warm, well-written letter of appreciation can make all the difference. Finally, saying "thank you" will provide big benefits over the course of your career.

PART IV

INTERVIEW SCRIPTS

For most job seekers, the crucial make-or-break moments come with the interview or string of interviews. Part IV will show you how to succeed in these high-stakes encounters by preparing intensely, creating a winning interview script, mastering Q&A (including both the most common questions and those wild-card quirky ones), and making your interview a standout performance. Following up and staying connected are also critical. Then, all you have to do is wait for the good news.

CHAPTER 12

Rock Your Research

YOU'VE WRITTEN YOUR RESUME and cover letter, and now you have an upcoming job interview. Nerves may set in as you wonder what they'll ask you and how you'll answer. Thinking about these things can make you anxious or even panicky. But don't worry. You can walk into that interview from a position of strength by doing your research. As we've all heard often, knowledge is power.

Prepare for that crucial meeting by deepening your knowledge in four areas: the company, the culture, the interviewer, and the job. Your research will make you come across as savvy and well prepared. And your exploration of those topics will enable you to ask good probing questions that will help you gain the insights needed to make the right decision about whether you want to accept an offer.

Researching the Company

Begin your research by studying the hiring company. This will show respect for that organization and elevate your discussion with the interviewer.

Chris Kowalewski, chief growth officer for Compass Group, which employs over 600,000 people, explained to me: "I want to know that job candidates have done research on us, so I'll ask them what they know about Compass—the operating company and the opportunity—and who they know in the organization, just to get a sense of how much research they've done. If they're not going to do due diligence on us, how are they going to do due diligence when they sell to prospective clients? Do they have the ability to drill down into the details of what a prospective client wants? Do they have the patience to do that? The temperament to do that?"[1] Kowalewski wants to make sure candidates are as inquisitive about Compass as they will be about prospective clients. He says: "I would expect a candidate to go read the annual reports at the very least. Read the chairman's letter to shareholders and articulate some really good questions around it. Ask, 'Why do you believe this direction is possible?' 'What in the past has indicated this path forward?'"

Before interviewing a candidate, Kowalewski even gives a job seeker an opportunity to meet with four or five people in his organization. These are not interviews per se; they're opportunities for the candidate to learn more about the company. And they give the job seeker a chance to ask probing questions. Such meetings may give the candidate fresh, new information. But if you are offered such an opportunity by an employer, realize that the employer is also gaining information about you—intelligence that may be passed on to the hiring executive. Put your best self forward and prepare to make a good impression.

By providing these pre-interview meetings, companies can expect that job seekers will be more knowledgeable and ready to pose insightful questions in the ultimate interviews. Kowalewski, in fact, expects a candidate's research to continue in the interview with him, and he looks more favorably on candidates that take notes with pen in hand. After all, until you decide to accept or reject an offer, you should be researching the company as much as they're researching you.

Jamie Dimon, chairman and chief executive officer of JPMorgan Chase, is similarly outspoken about the imperative of researching the company. Talking about job interviews, he observes, "Some people walk into your office, and they say, 'Gee, I'd like to know about the strategy of your company.' They didn't bother to read the chairman's letter I wrote, which is about 30 or 40 pages long." On the other hand, he notes that "other people walk in, and they know everything about the company." Dimon says that when a candidate researches the company, the discussion can go to a whole different level. And it's the people who have studied the company that Dimon wants to hire.[2]

During the nearly three decades I headed my company, what impressed me most were those job seekers who knew about our courses and could tell me why they were inspired to seek a position with our firm. When a candidate's only reference point was himself, I was turned off. One such job seeker came with tons of anecdotes about his brilliant stage career, but he never mentioned a thing about my firm—the company he was applying to. I couldn't wait for that interview to end.

Study everything about the company that you can find in the public domain—annual reports, executive speeches and presentations, media interviews, and social media sites, including the firm's website. Also, look at the company page on LinkedIn. Wrap your mind around what its leaders are saying—what their vision is. Ask yourself if the company's goals impress you. If so, why?

If not, why? How are they positioned in the industry? What's their strategic vision? Don't be afraid to ask anyone who works for that company serious, analytical questions. Bring yourself up to speed on every facet of the organization.

If you walk in with this knowledge, you will ideally be able to tell the interviewer, "I'm impressed with the direction your company is taking." Or "I was inspired by your president's speech." Or "I like the fact that you are a socially conscious firm." A fuller understanding of the company will also allow you to ask key questions in the interview and find out whether the job is a good fit for you.

A recent study of those interviewing for NFL head coaching jobs demonstrates the deep research undertaken by prospective hires. Anyone applying for this coveted role no doubt has a wealth of knowledge about the team and its players. But beyond that, consultants furnish candidates with detailed reports "that include the team's cap situation, team needs, scouting reports, and an explanation on what went wrong with the previous coaching staff."[3]

Suppose you're interviewing for an in-house job. Does that mean you can forego the research? Absolutely not! You'll need to make sure you're an expert on the company and that you can talk about its place in the market, its future, its people, and why you are committed to staying on with this firm. You'll also want to do deep research into the department you're applying to. What interests you about it, what is its reputation, and why do you want to be part of it? The good news is that if you are a strong performer and truly care about the company you're working for, you've probably internalized much of this knowledge. You can also ask any of your colleagues for further insights and get the inside scoop on any department.

Researching the Culture

Next, do your homework on the organization's culture. For job seekers, company culture has become more important than ever. In 2021, Workhuman IQ polled more than 3,500 employees in the United States, the United Kingdom, Ireland, and Canada and found that culture was the key determinant of whether an individual stays with a company. Workplace practices—such as appreciation, communication, inclusion, and flexibility— made all the difference, according to this study.[4] The "Great Resignation" (as the widespread hunt for new positions beginning in 2021 has been called) is being driven by workers who dislike the culture of their workplace and are actively searching for a more fulfilling environment.

If you're interested in employment in a new company, examine its back-to-work protocols. Do they encourage a return to the office, allow working from home, or permit a hybrid approach? Having this knowledge will allow you to discuss your fit with these options. If the policy is not clear or not to your liking, you can raise that in the interview.

Find out what the work environment is like. The Muse, an online career platform, offers photos of employees working in a variety of companies, from well-known firms like Siemens and Apple to fast-growing but less known companies like Gentle Dental. These photos are featured in the "Companies" section of The Muse's website.[5] They show the interior of offices, the way meeting rooms are set up, and where employees work and talk. That interior landscape can be all important. A young media professional I know found it impossible to work creatively when he joined a design firm because he was crammed in with other creatives at a long table. After a year of frustration, he quit and never looked back.

Also examine whether the company supports employees' mental health and well-being. Modern Health commissioned a wide-ranging 2021 study of more than 1,700 business leaders, HR leaders, managers, and employees with Forrester Consulting.[6] Of the study, Alyson Watson, the founder and CEO of Modern Health, writes in a *Fast Company* article: "64 percent of manager and nonmanager employees rank a flexible and supportive culture over a higher salary and are prepared to change jobs to find it." Watson further explains that "for some, a supportive and flexible culture means providing therapy and coaching to staff or investing in memberships for meditation apps. Many companies are also beginning to offer time off to help employees decompress and prevent burnout."[7]

Finally, look at diversity and inclusion practices. When Ellen Pao, author of *Reset: My Fight for Inclusion and Lasting Change*, took a job with the venture capital firm Kleiner Perkins Caufield & Byers (now Kleiner Perkins), she was told "diversity was important" for the firm. Her experience revealed the opposite and led her to file a lawsuit against the firm. In an interview with Stav Ziv of The Muse, she advises job seekers who value diversity and inclusion to take three steps.[8] First, look at who's in charge and how the company presents itself. If all the leaders look the same, that should be a red flag. Second, google the company name in combination with the terms *harassment*, *racism*, and *lawsuit* to see if they have been involved in any untoward situations. If they have, do you feel comfortable with how those controversies have been handled? Third, ask direct questions in your interview, like "How do you think about diversity and inclusion?"

Talk to friends or acquaintances who have worked for the

company you're interviewing with. Search LinkedIn for information. Check out Glassdoor for employee reviews. And study the firm's website for cultural cues. For example, if the website shows only senior executives, it's likely a top-down company. If it only shows white males or people with Anglo-Saxon names, that too should send up a red flag. Gather this intelligence and be prepared to discuss it in your interview.

If you are seeking a promotion within your company, think about the culture. Do its work from home policies align with yours? Do you get a good feeling about your colleagues and their values? Do you feel respected and believe that the culture of your firm is inclusive? Do the leaders live the values? One job seeker I know left her firm because management had not internalized the values. Authenticity was one of the company's values, so her boss would say, "OK, now I'm going to be authentic," before he shared something. It was all for show. These cultural dimensions should be researched before you decide to stay with your company.

Researching the Interviewer

Once you've studied the company and its culture, research the people you'll meet with. Anybody who interviews you will be impressed by the fact that you have taken time to get to know them in advance. Doing so will help you talk with them. You can probe further when you're with them.

When you have multiple interviews, research each person. Go to their LinkedIn profile, google them, and look into what specific work they have done. If you're meeting with a creative director of an ad agency, for example, check out their campaigns.

You will be able to say, "I love the campaign you guys did for Product X." If you're meeting with an executive in finance, you might say, "I see you're about to take the company public." If you are interviewing with a recruiter, you might mention an article the recruiter has written. The point is to show respect and interest.

Researching each interviewer will also enable you to ask intelligent questions. In an interview with an HR manager, you might say, "I understand from my research that employee satisfaction is very high in your organization. What do you see as the key to those excellent results?" Or, if you have a series of interviews for an HR position and you discover that everyone interviewing you would be looking for your support, you might ask each one, "How do you see HR collaborating with your organization and what specific goals would you have for us?" Their answers will give you a deeper understanding of the people you'll be working with. In short, research enables you to ask intelligent questions and get sound answers.

Researching the interviewer also has another advantage: the questions you ask about the interviewer's experience make the interview more of a dialogue and allow you to project greater confidence. Here's what one millennial, Fang Yu, told me about her first interview with the person in an advertising agency who would become her boss:

> I was applying for a strategist role, and a large part of being a good strategist is finding out how things work. Often a part of the role includes researching and interviewing customers—and I wanted to show that I had the confidence to do that. I asked the interviewer as many

questions as he asked me. I asked, "What's your favorite account?" "What's your day like?" "Do you function as a start-up or mature company?" This interaction made the interview very enjoyable and allowed me to project confidence—which was one of the reasons I got the job.

For an internal candidate, this research on the interviewer would involve asking the same types of questions. But finding out about the interviewer is so much easier when you're applying for an internal position because you can use inside intelligence. Beware, however, of falling prey to gossip, misinformation, or chatter about people you might be meeting with. Keep your outlook and your words positive.

Researching the Job

Finally, do your due diligence on the job itself. Having a good sense of the job inside and out and the challenges you'll face allows you to pitch yourself successfully—and prepare for the job should you land it.

Examine the job description and ask yourself what qualities and skills are demanded. Some job descriptions are filled with so much jargon that it's challenging to figure out what the position is about. If you don't understand the description, the job may simply be a jumble of responsibilities. Be wary of such positions. But if there is clarity, analyze the position advertised. You want to be able to present your strengths and the areas where you can contribute from day one. In areas where you don't have proven experience, you'll want to show how you'll develop those skills.

In many instances, the company expects the candidate

to bring new ideas to the table. That was made clear to Alex Burstein, a candidate for a position at US tech firm Calix. Her first interviewer said to her: "I want you to do a little research on us, on our culture, study our website, and come back and tell me what you think of what we have so far and what you would do in your new role as culture initiatives specialist." Alex told me:

> I went away and talked to a whole bunch of people. I called my brother, and my dad who is a therapist. I called a family friend who is a life coach, and I talked to my best friend, who runs all the leadership and training at Lululemon. I thought about who in my life are people who deal with people. I talked to them about leadership training, team workshops, keynote speakers, and women's health. I came back with all these ideas, and my future boss was like, "Wow, I can see that you are passionate, and you have lots of ideas." She then asked me to create a brief video about what I would do in the role.[9]

Companies want you to be knowledgeable about the job you're applying for. That benefits you and the company. Mike Hudy, chief science officer of Modern Hire, notes that firms are providing job candidates with more information than ever. Modern Hire works with over 300 large enterprises (including 47 of the Fortune 100 companies), and 20 million candidates a year are assessed and interviewed with its hiring platform. Candidates are given an online look at the job to make sure they truly understand the position. This can be a full description of the job or a day in the life of an employee who holds that position.[10]

Ideally, your research will enable you to position yourself as a perfect fit for the job—and talk about how you can contribute from day one. As chief growth officer for Compass Group, Chris Kowalewski looks for candidates who bring that energy. He told me: "If someone comes through the door and says, 'I've done my research, here's what I know about Compass, here's what I know about the job, here's how I would approach the first 30, 60, 90 days,' they'd probably get the job." When I asked Kowalewski what specific responses he was looking for, he replied: "There's not a single best answer. It's based on the research the candidate has done. Can they articulate a plan for the first three months?"[11] If you're in IT, it might mean building strong relationships and getting to know (and leading others) in the IT environment. If you're in sales, the first three months might involve building good relationships with clients, partners, and teammates, and mastering the sales platform.

An essay from The Muse titled "The 30-60-90 Day Plan: Your Secret Weapon for New Job Success" provides a great in-depth analysis of a 30-60-90-day plan and explains that this plan should contain your high-level priorities and actionable goals, as well as the metrics that will measure your success in those first three months.[12]

Even if you're not asked about how you'll perform during the first 30, 60, or 90 days, take the lead and provide those insights to your interviewer. You'll want to show what you will do for that company. As one successful job seeker, Michael Palombo, told me: "I always ask a future boss: 'In the next 12 months, what is your biggest challenge, and how can this role I'm applying for help you achieve your goals?'"[13] This question shows that the candidate wants to create value. It also gives the job seeker insight into the role and the reporting relationship.

Research is a powerful tool for preparing for interviews and asking questions in the interview. It will enable you to sell yourself successfully into that coveted role. Do your due diligence and research the company, the culture, the interviewers, and the job. Do as much research as you can in advance, and go into the interview with pen and paper and learn still more. This research will make you a star in the interview.

Next, you'll need to take all that research and put it into action. You can do so by developing a compelling interview script and astute answers to questions. If you do all this, you'll be on your way to a standout performance.

CHAPTER 13

Crafting an
Interview Script

YOU'VE LANDED THAT LONG-AWAITED INTERVIEW. Congratulations! Having come this far, you may be getting excited, telling yourself: "Don't blow it!" To ace that career-defining interview, you need this sense of urgency—and serious preparation.

It's essential that you have a clear, well-developed narrative for your job interview: an interview script. This will enable you to tell your story, whether you're applying for a new job within your company or outside it. Having that script means you know what you want to say about yourself and how you want to say it, and you have a set of arguments about your readiness for the role. It will enable you to sound clear-headed and help you avoid an all-too-common situation of job seekers who sit in fear of the interview and adopt a reactive mode, responding to questions but not leading the discussion in any way. That approach puts you at a huge disadvantage.

The interview script will not only give you a dynamic presence, but it will also form the basis for the Q&A prep discussed in the next chapter. Your interview script will transform your exchange from a series of disjointed comments to a larger story. It will allow you to be intentional and leave the room having gotten across all your major points. It's the key to acing the interview—and getting hired.

A Winning Interview Script

Getting job seekers ready for their high-stakes interviews has been one of the most rewarding aspects of my career, with the creation of the script as the centerpiece of that process. I have coached college and university students applying for their first position and C-level executives looking for a top job or a board position.

This preparation of a script has made all the difference. A millennial I helped apply for an internship at a major bank told me, "That interview script got me my first job; 100 percent!" Similarly successful was a vice president who sought a CEO position. Her biggest concern was getting nervous at interviews; I told her not to worry. The solution was to have a script that would make her feel powerful and confident. We created her narrative, and she landed the job.

This same scripting process will work for you whatever the format of your interview or level of the job you're applying for. You'll use the HIRE template to design your script. But before looking at those structural elements, keep in mind the following requirements of a good interview script.

It should be forward-looking. Focus the script on your desired new role—what you'll do for the company if they hire you. That's what the interviewer is looking for. Naturally, you'll talk about your experience and accomplishments, but that information must have a focus. You're not there to chronicle your career but to show why the positions you've held, and your education and skills, will make you the best candidate.

It should convey your excitement. The language you use should position you as enthusiastic about the hiring company and your role in it. You will want to say things like, "I am excited about this opportunity," "I look forward to becoming part of the team," or "I am keen to work on bigger, bolder projects in the US market." Ask about next steps. That shows you believe you're a good fit with the role and the expectations surrounding it. Conveying that you are already invested in the job illustrates your enthusiasm.

It should reflect personal characteristics discussed in chapter 2. These are authenticity, positivity, passion, confidence, impact, resilience, humility, respectfulness, and gratitude. Of course, you may not be able to cover all bases, but these are the qualities employers look for—and the more they enter into your script, the better.

It should be written out. The following discussion explores several approaches to creating an interview script. You may choose to create yours with full sentences or bullet points or slides or video. They all require that you formulate in words what you plan to say. This is critical if you want to impress. Knowing where you're going with your pitch is absolutely fundamental to speaking with clarity and confidence.

It should be internalized. There is no point in preparing a great script if you don't make it your own. You'll want to sound spontaneous, and the best way to sound confidently impromptu is to learn what you want to say, repeat it over and over again, and ask your family and friends to listen and give you feedback.

(See chapter 5.) If you practice, you'll internalize it, and it will sound natural.

Using HIRE to Structure Your Interview Script

These requirements are important, and they should shape your scripting. But to truly make your interview narrative persuasive, design it around the four elements of the HIRE template. Open with your hook or grabber, which sets the stage by showing your appreciation for the interview and your excitement about the company and job. Next, inspire with a main idea or message that conveys why you believe you are an ideal candidate for the position. Then, reinforce that message with proof points. These might be arranged chronologically or as a series of reasons, or as a situation/response structure. Finally, engage the interviewer with a call to action—look ahead to next steps, and declare yourself ready to take on the new role (and ask when you can expect to hear from the employer).

The five kinds of interview scripts we'll look at here are all built around this HIRE template. The first two (the word-for-word script and the bullet-point script) offer straightforward ways to prepare for an in-person interview. The next three (the PowerPoint script, demo script, and video script) are less common and may reflect the directives of the organization interviewing you. I've worked with job candidates who have used all five different approaches with great effect.

Keep in mind that whether you are applying for a job in your present company or in a new company, this level of preparation is a must. Even if you know the hiring manager or have met her at a company event, don't feel you can be more casual in your preparation. An interview is an interview and deserves deep thought and mastery of the material.

1. A WORD-FOR-WORD SCRIPT

One approach to preparing for the interview is writing out the main elements of your script in full sentences. Those sentences will guide you, and you'll hit the main points with well-chosen words. A candidate I coached for a CEO position used this approach—and it landed her the big job. This is her script that is structured using HIRE.

Hook—with a grabber
I believe in your organization—and its clean
energy mission.

Inspire—with a message
I'm confident I can lead your firm in implementing
this mandate.

Reinforce—with proof points
1. I will bring the leadership skills you are looking for.
   - As division head, I've led a talented team—with excellent results.
   - One of my key strengths is developing a strategic vision.
2. I'll be a strong spokesperson for your clean energy mandate.
   - I've done so at the national level.

- I've done so at the state level.
- I've built trust with local groups.

3. I have expertise in handling P&L—a requirement of any CEO.

Engage—with a call to action
I enjoyed the interview and appreciate your sharing so much with me. I'm excited about this opportunity and will keep my fingers crossed about the committee's decision.

In the interview, the candidate expanded on each of the subpoints. That was easy, since her sentence outline provided strong guidance.

2. A BULLET-POINT SCRIPT

A second approach to creating an interview script uses bullet points. A successful job seeker told me he likes this approach "because it feels more natural and spontaneous. That's why I prefer organizing my responses in sound bites." A script based on sound bites or bullet points provides a great set of memory joggers. It offers the key words that help the candidate remember the script's arguments. Here's a bulleted script that can provide a template for your interview script. In this instance, a college graduate is applying for an internship position.

Hook—with a grabber
I'm excited about this interview

Inspire—with a message

A great fit for my skills and interests

Reinforce—with proof points

1. Experience in business development—the online business I created in college

2. Strong aptitude for sales—not afraid to ask for the business

3. Familiar with your product line—keen to promote it

4. Have several strategies in mind (cold calls, referrals, social media marketing)

Engage—with a call to action

1. Appreciate your consideration

2. Would love to be chosen

3. Next steps?

Like the full sentence one, this bullet-point script keeps the job seeker on track. If you choose this approach, write out your sound bites, then learn them, and you'll go into the interview with a strong set of internalized messages.

3. A POWERPOINT SCRIPT

A third type of interview script is a PowerPoint presentation. If you're asked to do a PowerPoint talk, deliver one. If you're not asked to do one but want to blow the interviewers away, presenting them with a PowerPoint deck could be an example of creative, out-of-the-box thinking that will land you the job. Michael Palombo, a young job seeker who was applying for an internal job (a senior position at Twitter US) chose this approach. I asked him, "Did the interviewers request this presentation?" Michael said that they didn't, but he thought presenting one would be easier for the nine people interviewing him:

> It's stressful to run these interviews. So I built a master presentation that I customized for each interviewer. At the beginning of each interview, I said: "I prepared something that will let me take you through my story, but I'd be just as happy talking back and forth. It's totally up to you." And it worked. Every single interviewer said, "Do the presentation." It put me in a more advantageous position because I could tell my story clearly and with great examples. I timed it so I would speak for 21 minutes, and there would still be time for Q&A.

"How did it work out?" I asked him.

"My presentation got me to the second round of interviews—which I had hoped it would—and after that I was offered the job," he said. He explained how he constructed his job-winning talk:

> I began my presentation on a personal note. I said I was born and raised in Toronto and then showed a few photos of my life—one of my baby nephew and another of my two dogs—and I said I'd taken a screenwriting course during the pandemic. That part of the presentation showed who I am outside of work. That took a

minute and a half. That was my hook or grabber. Then I told them how my experience—particularly my success at Twitter Canada—made me the right person for this senior position.

"Ah, that's how you inspired—with a message," I said. "How did you go about reinforcing that message with proof points?" He explained:

I picked six wins I had chalked up in Twitter Canada, and for each interviewer, I chose the one or two wins that would be of greatest interest to them. And I built stories around each. So for example, when I was talking to an interviewer from the US sales division, I spoke about how I collaborated with our sales team in Canada. In all versions, I told them what we were doing, the tactics I used, and the results. Each example was like a micro story. Finally, I explained what I was looking for in my next role, emphasizing that I wanted bigger, bolder projects and was keen to develop new partnerships.

When I asked him how he ended his presentation, he said: "I asked each interviewer how in this role I could best support them and enhance their own contribution to the company. That was my way of engaging them with what I saw as collaboration."[1]

This presentation took the form of a story—and stories within the story. The narrative was developed using HIRE, with a hook, an inspiring message, reinforcing points, and engagement. It showed powerful thinking. It appealed to his audience and won Michael a new position and a much bigger opportunity in that role. He won the job as head of US content partnerships for Twitter in LA.

4. A DEMO SCRIPT

A fourth type of interview script is one that demonstrates your skills. Imagine yourself getting ready for that chance-of-a-lifetime career interview. Ask yourself: What can I do to really stand out? What can I do to ace this interview?

Why not introduce a short five-minute demo that shows your abilities in the area you're applying for? If you're a candidate for a sales position, show how you'd pitch a client. If you're applying for a software engineer position, demonstrate how you'd explain a new software product to senior management. If you're applying for a position as head of investments, demonstrate how you'd present financial results to the media.

Noah Yashinsky, a go-getter millennial whose first big job was in digital ad sales for Amazon, told me he had been working at a small company when the position at Amazon came to his attention. It was a dream job, but Noah knew he'd be competing against candidates from tech giants like Google, Facebook, Microsoft, and Yahoo. He told me: "I realized that since I didn't come in with a big brand, I'd need to go above and beyond in the interview—so I came into the five to seven interviews that had been scheduled for me with a mock proposal to a prospective Amazon customer, and at the beginning of each interview I said I'd like to do this mock pitch. Everyone who interviewed me was keen to hear the script."[2] Here's a summary of the pitch he delivered:

> We at Amazon know you're trying to draw more business to your product suites; we also know that last Friday—Black Friday—was super important to you. Your presence on our platform could have been bigger. We have a number of ad solutions that would help you drive more sales and expand your product reach. What do you say? Would you like to set up a meeting with me to discuss how we can make this happen?

When he finished his demo, Noah let each of the interviewers take away the four or five slides he'd used. He told me: "My mock proposal showed how I would pitch to a customer. It worked well because they not only saw me in action, but they got to take something away that was tangible and had my name all over it. They said this was one of the best interviews they had ever had. They were sold!"

The result? Noah got hired by Amazon—they actually created a job just for him. And it was a good move on their part. In the five years Noah has been at Amazon, he has consistently exceeded sales targets. He also was honored as the Global Quota Attainment Award winner two years in a row, and Jeff Bezos wrote him a letter of appreciation.

If you're applying for a job in sales, or any job that will take you into a marketplace, create a sales pitch to show your interviewer how you would sell your company's value. Your interviewer will be impressed that you took the initiative to understand the hiring company well enough to customize your pitch and demonstrate such impressive on-the-job skills.

5. A VIDEO SCRIPT

A fifth type of interview script is a video. Companies sometimes conduct video interviews where the candidate answers a list of questions. But there is another situation when a video will work wonders for you: sending a video in advance of an interview.

Alex Burstein, the young job seeker mentioned in the previous chapter, was asked by her future boss to create a video that would introduce her to the five people who would be interviewing her. She created a four-minute video of introduction and gave it to the people who would be interviewing her on Zoom. In it, she explained what the three cultural pillars in the company meant to her. Here's the opening of her video script, in which she makes a strong case for herself as a candidate for the position of culture initiatives specialist:

> Hi everyone, I wanted to introduce myself before we meet this week and tell you a little bit about myself. My name is Alex Burstein. I've been in the marketing and account management world for over five years now. I've always had a passion for humanity and helping people find the best in themselves and their surroundings. Empathy runs through my veins. I've been reflecting on the three cultural pillars of your company and wanted to share how I would try and bring each pillar to life as cultural initiatives specialist.[3]

This script has a hook (the first five sentences) and an inspiring message ("I've been reflecting "). Following this opening but not shown in this excerpt are three points in the body of her video presentation to reinforce her message. At the end, she engages with a call to action by saying: "I am very much looking forward to meeting with everyone and sharing some of my experiences—as well as answering your questions and asking a few of my own."

This video script focuses on Alex's vision of enhanced employee engagement, using the firm's three cultural pillars. In doing so, she clearly presents herself as a candidate who took the time to research the company. She shows how her life and values align with those of the company.

She created this video for her first five interviews and another video for her final interview. She even created a PowerPoint presentation for that last interview.

Did Alex get the job? Absolutely! After those videos, one presentation, and mastering 15 pages of notes about the company, she was golden. This is how to shine. She illustrates the qualities top job seekers demonstrate—they go above and beyond to land that coveted position.

Delivering Your Interview Script

The presentation, demo, and video scripts are set pieces. As for your written or bullet point script, these will be part of an interaction: a two-way discussion. In that interview, it's unlikely you'll get to deliver the full script all at once; there will be give and take with the interviewer. But your script will guide you—provide a road map—and you'll be certain to get your full story across during the interview.

Whichever of these scripts you use, preparing in advance will provide you with a direction and purpose that will enable you to exude confidence. You'll offer a full, persuasive picture of yourself and why you are ideally suited for the job. You'll leave the meeting having said what you wanted to say—and being extraordinarily persuasive in doing so. Preparing an interview script will also make it easier to create a set of answers to questions, which is the subject of the next chapter.

CHAPTER 14

Preparing for Q&A

FIELDING QUESTIONS IN A JOB INTERVIEW is a make-or-break skill. You may have the best credentials in the world, but if you can't talk about them intelligently and confidently, your interviewer will give you the thumbs down. Answering questions tests a candidate's agility, clarity, and readiness for the role. To impress the interviewer, prepare in advance. Before you enter the room, know how to answer the questions you're likely to get. This chapter discusses why preparation is crucial and how to prepare for any question that may come your way.

The Pitfalls for the Unprepared

Speaking spontaneously is an art; it doesn't come in the moment. If you rely on those spontaneous thoughts, you'll have little control over what you say. Stage fright can confuse our thought process. The better prepared you are for your interview, the more successfully spontaneous you will be. If you're unprepared, you'll encounter problems. Here are four.

#1 FREEZING OR SOUNDING AWKWARD

Go into an interview unprepared, and you may draw a blank or stumble when confronted with a question that surprises you. Your halting reply may sound like this: "Well, if you're asking about a problem I solved, there are many that come to mind, many I was involved in, let me think of the one that stands out, if I may."

One frustrated job seeker told me she had prepared for an interview by "reviewing a list of behavioral questions and trying to come up with answers." But "the interviewer only asked a few of those, and most of her questions were specific to the role, so I tried my best to answer them, but I got nervous and froze. It didn't go well. I haven't heard back."

There is also the awkwardness of one-word answers. One senior recruiter, Tejal Wagadia, highlights the dangers of awkwardly brief answers. She explains: "I might say, 'Tell me about the kind of position you have been looking for.' The candidate answers, 'technical positions.' 'What kind of technical position?' I ask. 'Project management.' When it feels like I'm pulling teeth," Wagadia explains, "I usually decide not to proceed with that candidate."[1] Those brief answers are often the result of not doing one's thinking in advance. Figure out what you might be asked and come up with inspiring answers.

#2 USING FILLER WORDS

Another pitfall for the unprepared is reliance on filler words. These empty expressions are annoying to listen to and show you haven't thought out your answers. You'll sound as if you're not interested in the job. Avoid plugging your answers with the following filler expressions:

- "Um" or "ah" makes you sound tentative. As early as the seventeenth century, "um" was identified as "a sound denoting hesitation."

- "Let me think" means you're asking permission to do what you should have done in advance.

- "Well" signals you're buying time. That won't inspire confidence.

- "You know" is meaningless because if the recruiter knew, he or she wouldn't be asking you this question.

- "Like" is a filler word that has become a habit with many speakers over the past few decades and is usually grammatically incorrect as well.

- "That's a good question" is a common opening reply and inappropriate because you're not there to evaluate the question, you're there to answer it. Telling an interviewer she's asked a good question can sound condescending.

- "That's a tough one" tells the interviewer you're in over your head—never a good sign.

All these expressions will turn a recruiter off, especially when used frequently during an interview. Prepare well, and you'll find no need for those empty phrases.

#3 RAMBLING

An unprepared job candidate may start talking, hoping something will come from a lengthy answer—in other words, they ramble. Suppose, for example, a candidate is seeking a job as a financial advisor and is asked in the interview to explain to a customer the plusses and minuses of investing in bonds.

Caught out, the job seeker might respond, "Yeah, well, bonds, I'd say, I mean I have never actually handled the bond portfolio, although I did take a course on investment strategies that included a chapter on bonds, so that was useful, and bonds are really a complex investment vehicle that often are issued by corporations and governments as debt, and they are sometimes bundled into funds—and they carry ratings, with junk bonds having a rating of BB+ or lower. So really, what I'd say . . . what was the question?"

With this answer, the interviewer is likely to conclude pretty quickly you are not the right person for the job.

#4 GIVING THE WRONG ANSWER

Unprepared candidates may also end up giving answers that are wide of the mark. A senior recruiter told me that she was hiring for a data scientist position. She said: "I had an interview with someone who was brilliant. We wanted him to lead our department. My first question was, what did a typical day look like for him in his current job." He replied: "I like to get into the work, I don't want to deal with the politics of anything outside data science."

The recruiter told me, "We had something else in mind. We needed a technical expert to head the department and also be able to go out there and explain to the leaders in the company how it worked. He was very micro, but we needed macro. He knew what we were looking for, but he hadn't thought it through, and that one answer did him in."

Preparation Is Key

Imagine you have an interview lined up, and you've got several days or more before it happens. The key to acing Q&A is preparation. Begin by listing the top questions interviewers ask (we'll discuss these in more detail in the next chapter), along with specific questions that apply to you. For example, if you have gaps in your resume, you'll be queried about this, or if you've switched careers, you'll need to be able to explain. There are also questions specific to the job you're applying for. If you're being interviewed for a position as HR manager, you're likely to be asked how you'd address retention issues. For a software job, you'd have to explore how you'd work with a team on app design. Then there are quirky questions you'll want to practice answering (more on that in chapter 16).

Finally, there are questions that your hiring firm may typically ask. Try to find out what these are. A senior manager I interviewed advised: "If you have career aspirations, you need to know what your desired company is looking for, find out from people who work there what they're likely to ask, then make sure in your current role or in school, you have the experience to back up your answers to these questions."

Know how to handle all types of questions. By the time you've thought out your answers to 15 or 20 questions, you'll find you're ready for most questions that come at you. Now, compose full sentence answers to the questions you've written down.

Once you've written down your answers, learn them as best you can by studying them in silence. Go over what you've written: line by line, word by word. Then, when you feel you've mastered them, rehearse them out loud. Enlist a friend, family member, or a coach to rehearse you. As you deliver your answers, don't try to make every word identical to what's written down. Your language will likely change. This is what makes your delivery sound spontaneous. But the thought structure will be similar to what you've burned in your mind. That will give your answers clarity.

Will this crafting and rehearsing of Q&A take time? Absolutely. Is it worth it? Ask yourself, "Do I want this job?" If you do, this prep work is more than worth it. A talented millennial at a top consulting firm said to me, "The people who receive high evaluations in our interviews are those who give great answers to questions. They've thought about their answers, and it shows."

You'll find that in preparing answers to specific questions, you'll become comfortable with the process of structuring your answers. You'll also be able to provide excellent answers to related questions you did not specifically rehearse.

Case Study: A Doctor Interviews for a Fellowship

Here's a good illustration of how this process works. I once prepared an MD for an interview for an emergency medical fellowship. The competition was stiff, and he was determined to win this fellowship, which would enhance his career. I asked him to write out all the questions they might ask. The list included ones that any candidate should prepare for (such as "Tell me about yourself" and "Where do you see yourself in five years?"). He also prepared ones that were specific to his chosen field of family and emergency medicine.

Here is a short list of his anticipated questions:

- Tell me about yourself.
- Where do you see yourself in five years?

- Why are you interested in emergency medicine?
- How might you contribute?
- What do you want to do in the future?
- Tell me about a problem you solved in your emergency rotation.
- Why are you a good fit for the program?
- Why do you need another year of residency?
- How do you see your career unfolding?

In all, he came up with a list of 25 questions—he was ready for the interviewers. He worked so conscientiously to prepare by mastering the design of the HIRE template that he was even able to use it to answer more personal questions. One such question was: "What experiences have led you to choose emergency medicine as a career?"

Hook—with a grabber
There were many.

Inspire—with a message
I've had an interest in emergency medicine since I was a child.

Reinforce—with proof points
1. My mom was a family physician. We had many discussions at our table about cases she was dealing with—and I was particularly impressed by the compassion she showed for her many patients who were in difficult straits.

2. I grew still more interested in emergency medicine while in med school. I assisted at an inner city doctor's office that handled a lot of emergencies and trauma cases.

3. After med school, I broadened my knowledge by working in a clinic that had many doctors. The specialities in that office included travel medicine, obstetrics, and geriatrics.

4. These experiences have taught me that my calling is to be a doctor who can compassionately treat patients in any medical emergency.

Engage—with a call to action
This fellowship would allow me to pursue a field I have always been interested in.

The scripts worked! This doctor received the fellowship. When you prepare, you'll outshine other candidates who have not practiced this discipline and who go into interviews cold. If you are asked some questions you haven't prepared for, you'll still be far ahead because the HIRE template will support you even when a question is unexpected.

Have Some Great Stories in Your Back Pocket

To support your answers, have some good stories to tell. You can see the effectiveness of such narratives in the young doctor's example, where the candidate told stories about his family and life. Include such colorful, personal accounts in your answers. They'll engage the interviewer and show how you've been successful, where you went above and beyond, and how you have distinguished yourself in various ways.

Donna Khawaja, who heads talent management for EY in Canada, discusses the need to portray yourself as exceptional in some way. In a conversation with Riva Gold, senior editor of LinkedIn, she says: "We tell candidates that come to us, to be yourself, show us what you're about, why are you different, why are you unique, and don't be shy about sharing that, because that's really what we look for." In short, Khawaja explains, "We look for unique experiences, unique skills, something that sets you apart."[2]

One senior manager who conducts interviews for a top consulting firm advises, "Be prepared to tell your interviewer about situations when YOU drove success, when you went above and beyond. When I hear a great story, I say, 'This person will succeed here.' So tell an incredible story, one that's unique and shows you went out and did something amazing. If someone went massively above and beyond what was required or expected at work or school, we know she'll do the same at our firm."

"Can you share such an inspiring story?" I asked.

"Yes. The one that comes to mind was told to me by an applicant from the University of Southern California. She had worked on a school committee advocating to the California government. One weekend, the group planned to lobby the California legislature, but not everyone could afford to go. So she organized a snap fundraiser, raised a few thousand dollars, and everybody was able to attend. That showed a tremendous amount of self-motivation, leadership, and problem-solving initiative. We hired her!"

"Are there some stories that don't work?" I asked.

"Yes. If somebody says, 'I was in my university's Math Club.' Or 'I attended a course on Excel Skills for Business.' That wouldn't do it for me. Unless they went on to show how they transformed the Math Club or used their new-found skills to carve out something new and exciting. I'd need to see that this person did something bold and independent. You see, much of the work we are hiring for involves independent thinking. And we look for people who are adept at finding solutions to problems."

"Was there such a story that got you hired?" I asked.

"Yes," he replied. "I had been working on the campaign of a US senator who was running for office against someone who had reached into her own deep pockets to raise money for her campaign. I saw this as a media opportunity and built an email campaign for my senator around the theme that one shouldn't have to be rich to win. This turned out to be the most successful email campaign for this senator."

These winning stories don't come to job seekers in a flash during the interview. You have to constantly be thinking about how to build stories for your next job interview. You have to come out of each job with a few good stories. All of them involve going above and beyond. You always need to be ambitious in this way.

Q&A preparation involves lots of hard work. If you commit to this process, you'll win your interviewers over. Each interview requires carefully crafted answers that are focused on that particular job, so be sure to focus on each job specifically—and give them your all.

Now let's talk about the types of questions you can expect—and how to develop answers to them.

CHAPTER 15

Mastering the Most Common Questions

FAST COMPANY ONCE ASKED ME to deliver a workshop for their annual Innovation Festival. The subject was "How to Answer the Interview Questions that Trip Everybody Up." I focused on the questions that come up again and again in interviews. These are topics that every job seeker should prepare for, and you'll want to have them down cold. Here are eight common questions with strategies for answering them. Each one provides an opportunity to tell your story using the HIRE template.

Question #1: Tell Me About Yourself

This question is the one that everyone asks—companies want to get to know you and see how you think about yourself. The challenge is that the question is so open-ended that you might fall into the trap of answering it with a meandering narrative, instead of presenting a clear, impactful story about yourself. Mikele Watters, a career coach and former Bank of Montreal executive, provides the key to fielding this one: "The answer to this question has to be focused on what the employer is looking for. An employer doesn't care what you can do; they care about what you can do for them."[1]

Think out your personal story—make sure its point is one that will help you land the job. Watters told me about how she was interviewed for a position in Bank of Montreal's Capital Markets group, a hard-driving, largely male bastion. She wanted to make clear she was tough enough to flourish in that world, so she shared this story with the interviewer:

> I'm driven and passionate and love a competitive environment. At the age of 35 I learned how to play hockey, and for the past 15 years, I have played competitive hockey equally well with men and women. I thrive in a competitive environment. That's why I believe I'm cut out for this role in your Capital Markets group. Some women might feel like outsiders, but I will feel right at home. And I look forward to the prospect of bringing my HR savvy to this capital markets arena.

Her answer shows she'll work well in that competitive arena. She got the job and did extremely well in it.

In answering this question, show something special about yourself that will serve your employer well in your new role. This might be your passion for your work, what drives you, your career vision, or your expertise. For example, you might say, "I'm a person who has built strong teams in a series of communications roles," and illustrate how you've done that. Or you might say, "If there's one thing that defines me it's my passion for leading people," and then show how you have led.

Find a single message about yourself—and drive it home. Suppose you're applying for a promotion in your current company's HR department, and you are asked this question. Here's a great answer, using the HIRE template:

Hook—with a grabber
My life does have a thread running through it.

Inspire—with a message
I love people, work well with them, and that's why I'm passionate about HR.

Reinforce—with proof points

1. I was outgoing and extroverted even when young. (Explain with an example.)

2. In university, I majored in psychology because I wanted to understand why people behave the way they do and the issues they might have in the workplace.

3. In my last two HR positions in this company, I've developed programs that make employees feel safe and engaged. I'm particularly proud of our mental health initiative.

4. Looking ahead, I want to continue to be part of this organization that values people, that is inclusive, and that gives employees the tools they need to succeed.

Engage—with a call to action
This position we are discussing would allow me to further strengthen our organization, whose

empathetic values I fully share. This is definitely a job
that excites me!

The speaker develops her message with proof points organized chronologically. The message could also have been
developed with reasons why she works well with people—
but the chronological approach allows her to show a lifelong
commitment to people and helping them, so it's an even more
powerful and well-structured answer this way.

Question #2: What's Your Biggest Weakness?

In answering this question, you don't want to sound like you
have a weakness that will hurt you in the job (e.g., "I don't work
well with people" or "I can't stand pressure"). But if you suggest
a weakness that's obviously a strength ("I'm extraordinarily dedicated"), you'll sound too goody-goody. Hiring managers will
quickly see through that approach.

One way to answer this question is to choose a quality that
seems to be a weakness but can be a strength: "I'm detail ori-
ented. That sometimes can slow me down, but in finance, it can be
an advantage." Or "I'm a perfectionist, and that can mean I push
myself too hard on projects." Perhaps your weakness is that you're
an introvert, and that causes you to keep to yourself. But you might
add, "I'm told there's a silver lining to this: introverts actually have
some excellent workplace advantages, given their superior ability
to listen, show empathy, and think before they speak."

An alternative would be to admit to a weakness, then show
how you're working on it by taking courses, building your skills,
or getting mentored. Here is a well-structured reply that does
exactly that, and it shows honesty and authenticity:

Hook
My biggest weakness?

Inspire
I'm so committed to the outcome of projects that I sometimes overmanage.

Reinforce
1. I am a real problem solver, so when I see one, I rush to suggest to my colleagues what the solution should be. This comes from the fact that I have been a specialist for so many years and I'm now in my first management role.

2. But I'm working on it! As part of my new learning curve, I make sure I ask my team members how they would fix the problem, and I've become a better listener. Fortunately, I have a mentor who is helping me with this.

Engage
I am feeling much more confident in this area and look forward to collaborating with a team in this new role.

Question #3: How Would You Describe Your Leadership Style?

If you don't have people reporting to you, or if you are junior—even an intern—you might be thrown off by this question. But the assumption underlying the question is sound: anyone can be a leader at any level and at any stage of their career. Take time in advance to think about how you would answer this question. You might lead by example, by doing work that inspires others, or by providing direction to others. Think of situations where you moved others to act, and be able to tell the story of how this happened.

Here is a script that shows how a junior staffer might answer this question.

Hook
People don't usually think of someone at my level
as a leader.

Inspire
But I do my best to inspire others by confidently sharing my ideas and building consensus whenever I can.

Reinforce
I remember one instance at a recent team meeting
where I was the most junior member present. We
were in a big discussion about how to move ahead
with a project that was not going well. With the group
seemingly at odds, I suggested another perspective. I
explained why I thought my proposed strategy would
work and volunteered to put together a plan. Everyone
was thrilled by this solution I had put forward. I prepared the plan, and it was implemented.

Engage
I value opportunities where I can have my voice heard
and make a difference that contributes to the success of my company. I would bring that leadership to
the new role.

Question #4: Where Do You See Yourself in Five Years?

In answering this question, you don't want to appear boastful—or sound like someone without a plan. Either extreme will turn your interviewer off. A senior executive once told me that she was startled when after asking this question, the job applicant looked her in the eye and said, "I want to be where you're sitting in five years. I want your job." She said that response was presumptuous and was a deal-breaker. But you'll sound undirected if you have no particular goal and say, "I'm not sure," or "We'll just have to wait and see." One ideal response is to set the bar high for yourself but stay open to possibilities. If you have a career goal in mind, you'll be perceived as someone with vision and drive.

Here is such a script.

Hook
I've studied BankCo and am impressed by the opportunities for advancement.

Inspire
I envision several possibilities—all of which would appeal to me.

Reinforce

1. The first would be taking on a more senior role in risk management.

2. The second would be building on my expertise and moving to a collateral area such as card or insurance services.

3. The third would be simply remaining open to new possibilities as BankCo evolves and responds to this rapidly changing environment.

Engage

So, I see myself in a range of positions that are all promising and that would all give me an opportunity to make a valuable contribution to your bank.

If you're applying for an internal position—seeking a step up in your career path—you'll want to show knowledge of how people progress in the organization and how they move from jobs like the one you're applying for to more senior positions. This requires internal intelligence and political savvy.

Question #5: Why Do You Feel Qualified for This Position?

In answering, you should sound confident but not boastful. As you discuss your readiness for the role, emphasize the contributions of your team and the support provided by your boss. Show the fit between your experience and the position. Include your education, the courses you've taken, job experience, and the mentoring you've received. Do your research so that you know a lot about the position, but don't assume you know everything about the job. Use language like "My understanding is that this role is . . ."

Here is one millennial's answer.

Hook

Yes, I absolutely feel ready to take on this role.

Inspire

My education, skills, passion, and experience make me a good fit for the position of financial advisor to high-net-worth clients.

Reinforce

1. I've just graduated with a degree in finance, so I'm very comfortable discussing financial planning.

2. I'm a strong communicator with finely tuned soft skills.

3. I'm passionate about helping people and would love the opportunity to work with your clients in this role.

4. I like the way your bank offers clients an integrated portfolio of banking, investing, trust, and estate planning services. I would be able to cross-sell to your clients.

Engage

I believe it's the perfect job for me (and I for it).

Question #6: Tell Me About a Problem You Solved

The key to answering this question is to describe the situation fully so the interviewer can see how you rose to the occasion and solved the problem. Be careful not to get so bogged down in detail that you lose your audience. After the introductory hook, get right to the point—your inspiring idea or message. Reinforce that message by first explaining what the problem was and then what the solution was. Be precise about what resources were required, how long it took, and the value you added. Make it a good story, and be sure you include others in the account. Here is an excellent response from an applicant for a senior communications position.

Hook
One problem I tackled involved my boss's presentations.

Inspire
He hated them—and working with him, I found a great alternative.

Reinforce
1. His slides—which he'd been using long before I came on the job—were information-based, and he's an idea guy. They just weren't working for him. They didn't convey his natural voice. And his audiences appeared to be bored.

2. So I suggested we replace slide-based speaking with a more informal, natural style, using note cards as prompts. This gave him the freedom to talk directly with his audience and improvise—which he was really good at. He loved this approach, and so did his audiences.

Engage
I'm now rehearsing him for digital events. Should I be hired for the vice president of executive communications position in our company, I would provide every executive with this same level of service, making sure they have the best material and training.

Question #7: Why Are You Leaving Your Current Company?

You don't want to look like someone who's dissatisfied or has been unceremoniously dumped, yet you need to explain your departure. Be honest, but keep your answer as positive as you can. There are several possible replies.

If you are leaving your current company of your own accord, explain the excellent opportunity you had for growth and your desire to reposition yourself within the industry. Don't get into negative territory. When I went looking for my second job, I did so to leave a bad boss who regularly called those of us on his staff "idiots." I didn't share that with my next employer in the job interview, of course. I said that I had learned a lot from my boss (which I had), and I loved working for that tech company. But I also said I was ready to move on to a more senior role (which I was), and the one we were discussing was perfect. I landed that next job.

Paint a picture of yourself as an aspirational employee who has been fulfilled in your current role but is ready to take on the next step in building your career. Talk about your accomplishments, your game plan for moving to the next level in your career, and how the job you're applying for will require the skills you have developed.

If you are exiting your present company because you feel the culture of your company no longer meets your standards, you can mention that—particularly if your prospective employer has a markedly different culture. Resignation rates are high, especially in companies that do not support employees' mental health or allow them to work from home. Present this reason as part of your enthusiasm for the new position.

If you've been let go or chose to leave because of the COVID-19 pandemic or some related reality, say so—that's totally acceptable. Emphasize how much you've gained from that last position. If the pandemic made you want a different kind of work, that too could be something to share. And if you took a course or gained new skills during your employment hiatus, talk about what you learned. Even volunteering at a food bank deserves a mention. As Andrew Fennell writes in a *Fast Company* article, "People who volunteer are often thought to be caring, compassionate, selfless, driven, and reliable; these are also great traits in an employee."[2]

Finally, if you were fired, work out an answer that does not put you in a bad light. Don't lie or present a false picture—but don't air the dirty laundry behind the firing. For example, you could explain: "The company downsized and cut our entire department. That decision was made despite the excellent results we have achieved during the preceding four quarters." If you were fired because of poor chemistry with your boss, bite your tongue and say something less damaging, like "I had outgrown my job." Complete disclosure may feel good in the moment, but it will cut your chances of an offer. Always put as bright a face on that reality as you can.

Here's one response to "Why are you leaving your current job?"

Hook—with a grabber
The pandemic changed my approach to work.

Inspire—with your message
My decision to leave HomeCo reflects my interest in working for an insurance company, like Mutual Life, that offers a hybrid work environment.

Reinforce—with proof points

1. I valued my eight years at HomeCo, where I helped the actuarial department become an industry leader.

2. During 2020 and 2021, I found myself more productive and happier working from home, but unfortunately, HomeCo no longer provides this option.

3. One of the strong reasons I'm attracted to Mutual Life, along with your excellent reputation, is the hybrid work environment you offer.

Engage—with a call to action
For these reasons I'm very interested in joining the team at Mutual Life.

If you're applying for an internal position, emphasize not only that you are excited about the job but that you are in sync with the culture, the work-from-home policies, and the inclusive leadership practices. Carry the torch for the company and show you are a believer.

Question #8: Why Is There a Gap in Your Resume?

You need to be upfront about any significant gaps in your resume, but don't be embarrassed or apologetic. Jane Fraser, CEO of Citibank, earlier in her career chose to work part-time after being named a partner at consulting firm McKinsey. She said the decision to carve out time with her kids was critical to her later professional achievements. "I'm so glad I did it," she said in a *Fortune* interview. "I honestly don't think I would be here today if I hadn't."[3]

If an interviewer asks you about a gap, focus on the things you learned while you were away from the workforce. If you upgraded your skills, emphasize that. If you took off time to be with your family or to volunteer for a charity, highlight your compassionate side. Don't apologize for that decision. Life is full of adventures. Show that this was one that taught you something—and made you a better person and prospective employee.

Here's a worthy script:

Hook
I am glad you asked about this gap in my resume.

Inspire
I took time off to be with my young children and upgrade my skills.

Reinforce
1. I had time to nurture our three kids and give them the attention they deserve.

2. I also received certification in social media marketing, which will help me in the position I'm applying for.

3. I even became the facilitator for a group of mommy bloggers, and helped several people reach audiences of over 500,000 followers.

Engage
I'm recharged, have a broader skill set, and am ready to commit fully to this next career role.

These eight questions are some of the most frequently asked. Other common questions are either variations on these themes or close enough that you'll be able to use the material you prepared for the eight. Here are some examples of how your preparation will help:

- **How do you like to work?** This might be covered in discussing why you left your last position or how you explain a gap in your resume.

- **When let down by a teammate, what do you do?** Your answer on leadership style should help you answer this one.

- **Why do you want to work for us?** You've produced good material for this answer in discussing why you left your last job and why you feel qualified for this position.

The questions discussed in this chapter are classics—so study these examples and use them as models for your own.

Learning to create smooth and persuasive answers is a skill, like any other. Write out potential questions and your answers, and rehearse them so you don't have to rely on notes, even during virtual interviews. If you do all this, you'll be able to deliver clear, structured responses and do so with conviction. That will make all the difference.

Next, we'll look at some of the quirkier questions that might pop up in an interview and how you can prepare yourself for those as well.

CHAPTER 16

Being Quick with Quirky Questions

MY SON BEN TOLD ME that a creative director in advertising once surprised him by asking in an interview: "Hey, what's your favorite pizza place?" They were looking over Ben's portfolio and discussing an ad campaign Ben had done for a pizza company. Deep into the discussion of Ben's artistic talents came the question about his taste in pizzas. Ben realized, as he put it, that "he was sussing out my personality. Making sure I could handle the to and fro of a creative environment." He answered by giving three or four pizza places he likes.

However well prepared you are for your interview, inevitably some questions will take you by surprise. You should expect at least one curveball. If you're not ready for it, you might flub it. You may feel the interviewer is trying to trick you—but that's not the case. These questions are designed to get you to open up, to show how quick you are on your feet and whether you like to have fun. Job expert Amanda Augustine notes that interviewers "purposely want to force a candidate 'off-script' in order to get a better read on [them]."[1]

Quirky questions show how you perform under pressure—and how creatively you think in topsy-turvy situations. Given the unpredictable world we live in, recruiters and hiring managers are increasingly asking these questions to find employees with agility, resilience, and the ability to think quickly. It happens even in NFL interviews of candidates for head coach. Miami Dolphins executive Mike Tannenbaum has been known to ask, "If you could invite three people to dinner, dead or alive, who would they be?"[2] This chapter will help you field such quirky questions by responding with poise, clarity of thought—and an answer structured by the HIRE template.

Handling the Unexpected Questions

Even if you can't rehearse the way you would for standard interview questions, you can follow these four guidelines when oddball questions come barreling your way.

1. EXPECT THE UNEXPECTED

Go into the interview expecting a few surprises. Every company has its own favorites. Warby Parker, the eyeglass designer and manufacturer, looks for creative types. CEOs Neil Blumenthal and Dave Gilboa want to hire people who will "inject fun and quirkiness" into their company. So, they ask candidates: "What was a recent costume you wore?"[3]

Apple poses some of the most inventive queries. Interviewers there have been known to ask: "If you have two eggs, and you want to figure out what's the highest floor from which you can drop the egg without breaking it, how would you do it?"[4] There are many answers to this question, but a simple response would be to start on the first floor, see if it breaks, if not, go to the second floor, see if it holds up, and so forth, climbing higher and higher until it does break when dropped.

Amazon has challenged candidates with this question: "We're a peculiar company. What is peculiar about you?"[5] Microsoft asks, "How would you move Mt. Fuji?"[6] Nestlé poses this one: "If you were a brick in a wall, which brick would you be and why?"[7] Other questions high on the quirky scale might include "If you were a tree, what kind would you be?" or "What flavor of ice cream do you see yourself as?"

As companies place a higher emphasis on resilience in this post-pandemic world, they will look for answers to quirky questions that show you can deal with the unexpected with grace and wit.

2. CHOOSE ANSWERS THAT ILLUSTRATE YOUR CORE VALUES

When answering quirky questions, keep in mind your message and goals. You've come into the interview knowing what you offer. It might be that your strong background in human resources makes you the best candidate for this job or that your years in financial technology have made you a problem-solver who deserves this promotion. A quirky question may appear to pull you impossibly far from that message— but make it stick.

Your answer should illustrate your values. For example, if you're asked to solve problems while on Mars, your first response might be to show concern for the safety of your team, given that the red planet provides such an inhospitable environment. That response demonstrates your leadership qualities and emphasizes that you're a team player.

The question about which brick in a wall you'd like to be can elicit how you see yourself in relation to others. An aspiring CEO might want to be one of the highest bricks, one that the others look up to. An entrepreneur might want to be the first brick laid—a brick upon which the others find their purpose and future.

If you are asked, "What kind of tree would you be?" view it as a fun question whose answer can reflect your personality. You might respond that you'd be the mighty oak because you're a seasoned leader—and you could expand upon that by adding that just as the seeds of a mighty oak live inside the acorns that surround it, you've mentored many younger folks. Or you might suggest that you'd be an apple tree that produces fruit and adds beauty to the world when it blossoms every spring. If you're an intern or just out of university, you might choose to be a seedling, newly planted and ready to grow.

If an interviewer tells you that the company is peculiar and asks what is peculiar about you, you might respond that you don't see yourself as peculiar, but you do look at the world differently from most people. You challenge conventional thinking and explore alternatives. This, you believe, will make you an asset to the company.

Let your imagination run wild with these puzzlers and have fun, but keep in mind that these crazy questions are also serious ones for the interviewer. There are no right or wrong answers, but your imaginative response should reflect your values and core beliefs.

3. STAY COMPOSED

When these questions come your way, keep your cool. Don't screw up your face or respond with nervous body language. Nor should you comment on the question with "Wow, that's a whopper of a question!" or "Where did that one come from?" If these are the first words out of your mouth, you'll sound caught off guard. Instead, take a deep breath and pause when one of those wild questions comes your way. You need time to collect your thoughts, so don't rush to answer and get all garbled up in your thinking. Take your time, but don't overthink it. Just stay grounded and deliver a thoughtful answer.

4. DON'T LOOK FOR FEEDBACK

When you're through answering a quirky question, you may wonder if you were too off-base with the answer, and you'll probably feel a little weird. But don't ask for feedback. If you look for praise or positive reinforcement from the hiring manager or recruiter, it will suggest that you were unnerved by the question or unsure of your answer.

Instead, smile when you've finished and show you're comfortable with your quirky answer and the values you have expressed. This will demonstrate your comfort in dealing with even the most outrageous situations that might arise at work. And these days, demonstrating resilience is high on every employer's list.

True Examples of Quirky Q&As

When I published a *Fast Company* article that featured these quirky challenges, I received a deluge of responses from readers who shared the nutty questions they'd been asked and (in some cases) the answers they gave. Here's a short list drawn from that correspondence. These answers provide excellent guidance for how you might answer quirky questions.

QUESTION 1: IF YOU WERE AN ANIMAL, WHICH ONE WOULD YOU BE?

One reader answered that she would be an octopus "because I'm extremely organized and know what is going on around me." Another identified with a swan because "I am serene on top and paddling furiously underneath where no one can see my efforts." Still another suggested he'd be a duck because "I would be good at any job you give me: I can fly in the air, swim in the water, and walk on the land." Even a rhino makes the cut: one person said, "I have rhino hide; not much bothers me." All these job seekers scored well by having fun, showing authenticity, and finding qualities that presumably fit the role they were applying for.

QUESTION 2: CAN YOU PERFORM UNDER PRESSURE?

A no-frills answer might have been, "Yes, I handle workloads well and am committed to meeting tight deadlines." But the candidate who shared this story was much cleverer than that. He responded: "I don't know that one, but I could have a fair crack at 'Bohemian Rhapsody.'" He was riffing that the recruiter asked him to perform a song called "Under Pressure." Depending on the situation and the interviewer, this might be too clever a response. Be careful to judge whether the interviewer will get your witty reply and won't feel you're making fun of the question (or the questioner).

QUESTION 3: WHAT DO YOU THINK OF WALES?

The job seeker replied, "The country or the mammals?" This answer is super smart but again, read your audience to make sure your answer will be well received. Some interviewers would get a kick out of those humorous responses and be impressed with the quick wit of the candidates, but others might not flow with a response that answers a question with a question. They might expect you to figure out what was meant. It's about using your imagination.

QUESTION 4: CAN YOU TEACH ME HOW TO DO SOMETHING?

Here's a question that requires you to think on your feet and respond quickly to an unexpected challenge. After all, who plans to offer a tutorial in their interview? The interviewer who shared this question said that the last job candidate to whom he posed this question gave him a lesson in how to put on makeup. He wanted to see if she could clearly explain something that was known to her. Her choice of a topic was perfect, too, because putting makeup on others is what this candidate would be doing in her new role.

QUESTION 5: TELL ME SOMETHING I DON'T KNOW ABOUT YOU

This question is challenging because you have to reach beyond your resume and interview dialogue and share something that's more personal but not *too* revealing. The job candidate who related this story to me hit the jackpot. She told the interviewer that she had just started kickboxing. As it turned out, he was really interested as he did that himself. She got the job.

QUESTION 6: HOW MANY FISH COULD FIT INTO AN AVERAGE-SIZED SUITCASE?

A financial executive was interviewing for a senior accounting role when this question was posed to him. Imagining smelly fish in his suitcase, he replied: "If that were to be part of my job, I'd require extra pay and a clothing allowance." The candidate said, "There followed a short silence whilst my interviewer tried to determine whether I had taken his question too seriously or was batting his daft question back at him. I wasn't offered the job." A better approach would have been to have fun with this question, explaining how in good accountant fashion, he would tally up the number of fish needed to fill the suitcase.

QUESTION 7: DO YOU TELL A VEGAN ABOUT MEAT IN THE SOUP?

A reader who interviews job candidates asks this question: "Suppose you have a dinner party and serve vegetable soup that has lard, a meat product, in it. An important business guest remarks that the soup was delicious, and as a vegan, she's grateful you served it. What do you do? Do you tell the guest about the ingredients in the soup or remain quiet?" How you deal with this situation reflects your character and moral compass.

If you get such a question, don't stammer and freeze up, as this interviewer says some candidates do. Doing nothing is also not a good answer. The sales executive who poses this question says he wants future employees to demonstrate empathy and creativity. An ideal answer, he said, might be to quietly and privately share this information with the guest along with an apology that you hadn't realized her preferences.

QUESTION 8: WHAT DO YOU THINK YOUR FRIENDS WOULD SAY ABOUT YOU?

This is an intriguing question that deserves a serious answer. Don't respond, as one person did, and pronounce it "a weird, stupid question" or demand, "Why don't you ask them?" That's a good way of ending the interview and your chances of getting the job. A much better alternative would be to identify a quality that you believe you manifest and that will serve you well in your new role. For example, you might say, "They see me as honest and forthright," or "They would say I am resilient." Then explain why.

QUESTION 9: WHAT DO YOU THINK OF YOUR PARENTS AND BROTHER?

Questions about family and your personal life can cross the line. An interviewer for a financial services company fired three such questions at an applicant for a trainee position. "Your parents didn't go to university—how does that make you feel?" came first, followed by, "Your brother is a doctor, and you just studied English—how does that make you feel?" Finally, the interviewer asked, "You're the only female interviewee I've asked to see today—how does that feel?"

These three questions reflect poorly on the interviewer and the company. They have an edge to them and don't necessarily deserve a positive response. You learn about a company in these encounters, just as the company learns about you. You may choose not to answer such questions, even if that signals your displeasure with this process and your desire to get away from this company. If you do choose to answer—as this job seeker did—say you are proud of your parents. Then say you're proud you have an English degree because this will give you an advantage in the business world where soft skills are so important. As for being the only female interviewed that day, say you're glad the bank is committed to hiring more women in management, and you look forward to the prospect of being one of them.

It is illegal for companies to ask job seekers about the following:[8]

Age or genetic information

Birthplace, country of origin, or citizenship

Disability

Gender, sex, or sexual orientation

Marital and family status, pregnancy

Race, color, or ethnicity

Religion

Don't feel obliged to answer questions in these areas. Remember, you're interviewing the company at the same time they are interviewing you. If someone asks about any of these subjects, you can reply by saying, "I'd prefer not to get into that area," or "These are private matters." You'll probably say to yourself, "This is not a company I want to work for." Fortunately, questions on these taboo topics are posed much less often than they once were.

• • •

If you want further insight into answering off-the-wall questions, you may wish to consult William Poundstone's three books that discuss the art of answering unusual questions:

- *How Do You Fight a Horse-Sized Duck?: Secrets to Succeeding at Interview Mind Games and Getting the Job You Want.*[9]

- *Are You Smart Enough to Work at Google?: Trick Questions, Zen-Like Riddles, Insanely Difficult Puzzles, and Other Devious Interviewing Techniques You Need to Know to Get a Job Anywhere in the New Economy.*[10]

- *How Would You Move Mount Fuji?: Microsoft's Cult of the Puzzle—How the World's Smartest Companies Select the Most Creative Thinkers.*[11]

Answering and preparing for quirky questions can be fun. Don't take them too seriously, and don't try to find the "right" answer to any of them. The secret is to think of this part of the interview as a game in which interviewers are looking to see how you demonstrate your values, flow with the punches, and show enthusiasm and creativity.

Now that you've discovered how to prepare for your interviews, we'll explore how interviews are conducted (CEO style), and how to put your best foot forward in these high-stakes situations that will shape your career.

CHAPTER 17

Top Talk: What CEOs Look For

FEW JOB SEEKERS CAN EXPECT to be interviewed by the world's top CEOs like Mary Barra of GM, Tim Cook of Apple, or Jamie Dimon of JPMorgan Chase. Even those who have stepped away from the CEO role—like Indra Nooyi of PepsiCo or Sara Blakely, who founded Spanx—remain daunting presences in the world of job seekers.

While you likely will never have the opportunity to be interviewed by these CEOs, in this chapter you'll learn what they look for when they hunt for best-of-the-best talent. You'll discover what they expect when they hire and how to demonstrate those same talents in your job interviews. In short, view this chapter as a mentoring opportunity and take away new ideas about the qualities you would like your interviewers to see in you—qualities that the most rigorous interviewers will expect of anyone seeking employment with them.

What Mary Barra Looks For

Mary Barra, CEO of General Motors, challenges interview candidates with three closely related questions: What three adjectives would your peers use to describe you? What three adjectives would your boss use to describe you? And what three adjectives would those working for you use to describe you?[1] Those queries test a candidate's ability in several areas.

To begin with, they show the interviewer how self-aware a job seeker is. If you're applying for a job, you want to show the person interviewing you that you know what others would say about you, and that you are comfortable with the words they would use to describe you. In preparation for your next interview, think about what these adjectives might be. For example, suppose your boss says one day, "Thanks for getting this report in to me on schedule." Does that mean she thinks of you as a good worker? Or as organized? What other words would she use to describe you? And what about your direct reports or your peers? You need a thoughtful response, and it will be too late if you don't think of this before the interview.

Barra's questions also test how consistent a candidate is. As Barra puts it: "If you're hiring for integrity, you don't want people to manage up differently than they manage down, and you want people to work just as well with their peers and superiors as they do with their subordinates. This consistency is the key to empowering teams."[2] The secret is to be able to say that the same descriptors would be used by your boss, your colleagues, and your direct reports. If your boss sees you as a strong, confident leader, do those reporting to you see you the same way? Do your peers share that perspective? Ideally, yes.

Barra's questions also help an interviewer assess the soft

skills of a job candidate. If you tell your interviewer that your boss, your colleagues, and your team would say you're "empathetic," "supportive," and "inspiring," you'd have a good crack at a leadership role. But be honest, because you'll probably be asked to explain why others see you that way, and it's important to be prepared to answer.

Barra's questions also test a job candidate's readiness for the role. If you're asked some version of what Barra asks, the qualities mentioned in your answer should align with the job description. If you're applying to be a software programmer, you might want to say that your colleagues see you as "bright" and "technically savvy." If it's an HR job, you'd like to be known as "caring" and "people-focused." Be truthful, but also be mindful that the recruiter will make the connection between how others see you and your suitability for the job.

A great answer to Barra's three-in-one question will show you at your best. Barra says that one of the reasons she likes this question is that "you learn a lot about a person by the way they answer, given they have to think on their feet."[3] In fact, research indicates that anyone who can easily speak in impromptu situations is considered to be more charismatic than someone who fumbles.[4]

You might not get the exact set of questions Barra asks, but you may be asked, "How would your colleagues describe you?" Have your answer ready.

What Tim Cook Looks For

Tim Cook, CEO of Apple, looks for many qualities in job candidates—including grit and curiosity. But most importantly, he says he seeks job candidates who "won't accept the status quo, people who aren't satisfied with the way things are."[5] In short, he looks for people who "Think Different," as Apple's famous mantra advises.

You know you have this quality if you see things that can be improved and have the courage to take action. When Cook accepted the position at Apple he said it was because "I looked at the problems Apple had, and I thought, you know, I can make a contribution here."[6] His task was to overhaul Apple's manufacturing and distribution. His determination to fix Apple's problems involved a huge career risk for him. When Steve Jobs offered him a position in 1998 as senior vice president of Apple's worldwide operations, the company was on the skids. Cook had a secure job at Compaq, at that time the world's largest seller of personal computers. But he took the plunge and never looked back.

As an entrepreneur who founded a company in 1988, I can relate to this quality of acting when things can be improved. As a CEO speechwriter, I saw that many other executives had to craft their own talks and didn't know how, nor were they good at delivery. I thought that teaching them how to do this would make an excellent business. When I decided to take this bold step, many naysayers told me, "You have a good job with a bank. What more could you want?" I ignored their advice, and it's one of the best decisions I've ever made.

As a job seeker, you'll want to look back on your career and see where you've had the courage to challenge the status quo— it's a good attribute to keep in mind going into an interview. When you're asked during your interview, "Are you a person who accepts the status quo?" you'll have a great answer and an inspiring story to tell.

Go prepared to show how you challenged the status quo. Cook observes, "We [at Apple] look for people who really want to change the world and put all of themselves into doing it."[7] Cherish opportunities to be daring.

What Jamie Dimon Looks For

Jamie Dimon, chairman and chief executive officer of JPMorgan Chase, is a powerhouse who holds job seekers to the highest standards.

One thing he looks for in candidates is deep knowledge of his company. In an interview at Stanford University, he explained that some people arrive for an interview and they ask about things they should already know from their research, while others know what the company is doing. "So when we have a conversation, they are actually enhancing your life rather than the other way around."[8] In short, Dimon looks for prospective employees who do their homework and study the company—and, based on that information, have a thoughtful dialogue about how they can contribute.

Another thing Dimon looks for in interviewees is character. As he puts it, "Character is a sine qua non. And by character I mean they tell the whole truth and nothing but the truth, and they don't shade the truth." These people adhere to the highest principles. The clarity they provide "helps a company know what it's trying to accomplish." Dimon's advice will serve you well in all your interviews. Doing your research and showing character: What could be more fundamental?

What Indra Nooyi Looks For

PepsiCo's former chairperson and CEO Indra Nooyi has tons of good advice for job seekers, and her directives represent forward-looking insights for candidates when interviewed.

In her book *My Life in Full: Work, Family, and our Future*, she tells the story of how she has always looked to hire a diverse workforce and how recruiters should keep that global perspective in mind. After joining PepsiCo, she writes, "The team I took on lacked international diversity." So "I asked our internal recruiter for more diversity in the next group. Four months later, he proudly introduced me to the latest hires. I was amused and dismayed. They were all Canadian."[9]

She didn't give up. "I sat down with the hiring team and specified exactly what I meant by diversity. The following year, they did deliver, with an excellent group of truly global hires." Today's candidates should be aware that diversity is increasingly important to hiring executives. Seek out those executives who are so enlightened, as Nooyi was in this story, and you'll be working for a company that values inclusiveness.

Beyond that, Nooyi tells job seekers who want to build their careers to "become visible to people outside your work group. People should be saying 'you know she really did a fantastic job with this brand, I wish she'd work on my brand.'" And if you want to move up, she says, "show up at industry forums, speaking on major topics." Show that "you're not just thinking about the issues facing your company and your industry in isolation. But while you're doing your job, you're thinking about what's changing in your industry." She also encourages people who want to get ahead to do lots of reading: "Read, observe, watch, and from that you have to derive your own perspective about your industry, what's changing in the economy, and what kind of thinking can you bring." Bolstered by that insight, "When you go to industry meetings all of a sudden people are inviting you back. They want to hear what you have to say."[10]

Noori wants you to know that careers are built on knowing what is happening within your company, your industry, and the world. Any job candidate needs that depth and breadth when going into an interview—whether for an internal job or a new company or industry. Who knows, if you keep a high enough profile as a savvy thinker, you might even be approached by top-level industry suitors.

What Sara Blakely Looks For

Founder of women's intimate apparel company Spanx, Sara Blakely says that "the first things I look for when I'm hiring for a position of leadership are passion and intelligence. Probably 70 percent of my decision to hire someone is based on the feeling I get about him or her, and 30 percent has to do with the details of the job." When she hired a CEO, she said, "I was looking for somebody who had a real depth of knowledge in innovating products and in the supply chain."[11]

She further explains: "When it comes to the 70 percent—the reaction I have to someone—I want someone who's really smart, quick, and scrappy, who sees life as a glass half-full. I also believe you can learn the most about a person by the questions he or she asks or doesn't ask. So I let the candidate ask. I make sure I'm quiet for more than half of the time during our interview, and I also make sure there are a few awkward moments of silence. You usually hear the best stuff in those moments." That's sound advice for any serious job candidate. Watch for openings in the conversation to ask smart questions.

Blakely is so interested in the personal side of the candidate that she says: "I also had [ex-CEO] Jan Singer meet my husband, and I wanted to meet her husband. We had dinner. Meeting someone's significant other lets you see a dimension of him or her that you wouldn't necessarily encounter in an interview. You're meeting someone's chosen life partner. I've never disqualified a job candidate because a spouse was wrong. But my husband loved Jan right out of the gate. He looked at me and said, 'She's a powerhouse.'"

If you as a job seeker have an opportunity to meet teammates and even family members of your interviewer, seize the occasion, and bring enthusiasm and confidence to the gathering. Show you're a powerhouse! And even if you don't get this opportunity, realize that many interviewers like Blakely want to bond with you during the interview. They want to connect with you, and being able to do so may even be the deciding factor. Open up, be yourself, and enjoy the meeting.

• • •

All of these CEOs have one thing in common: they are evaluating people for who they are and what values they bring. Barra wants to know the words that define how others see the candidate. Tim Cook wants people who will change the world. Jamie Dimon wants character. Indra Nooyi wants someone who is driven to understand a company and its place in the industry and economy. Blakely wants passion and intelligence. In short, they are looking at *who the person is*. As you move up the ladder, you will be assessed by who you are, not what you can do. Study the culture of the company to figure out what perspective the CEO might have. Even if you're not speaking to the CEO, ask yourself what perspective your interviewer might have. Then go for it!

CHAPTER 18

Delivering a Standout Performance

AWESOME! YOU'VE MADE IT to the interview stage—and are one step closer to a job offer. The stakes are high, so you'll want to deliver a standout performance.

You've done all the prep work. You know the qualities you want to project. You've researched the company, its culture, the interviewers, and the job. You've prepared answers to the questions you might be asked and created a set of probing questions yourself. You've written out and rehearsed your interview script. And with it all, you have an amazing story to tell about yourself. Now it's time to deliver a star performance. To do that, study the following eight guidelines that apply to every kind of interview—whether by video, in-person, one-on-one, or in a group.

Here's to your success (and to the culmination of our journey together).

#1 Get the Tech Right

Webcams, microphones, videos, and virtual conversations have become the mainstay of interviews—and they likely are here to stay.

With a virtual interview, you'll want to be tech-savvy. There's no communication if you're accidentally muted or your camera is off. Invest in the highest-speed internet available, a fast computer with extra processing power, and a good microphone and camera. In her book *Presenting Virtually*,[1] Patti Sanchez suggests that you make these basic upgrades. Before your interview, do a trial run. Become comfortable with the platform the hiring company will be using. Get feedback on whether you're looking into the camera and whether your voice sounds strong.

If you're sending a video, make sure it sounds and looks professional—even if you're using your own equipment. One job seeker blew me away with the video she had created and sent to the VP who would be interviewing her. I commented on the smoothness of her delivery and the force of her gestures. She told me she achieved this stage presence by creating a homemade teleprompter, using a cell phone on a tripod above her computer. She used one hand, below the camera view, to scroll through the text on her laptop. And when she wasn't scrolling with that one hand, she'd include it in her gestures so that she looked like she was just talking and gesturing naturally with both hands.

Another possibility, if you're speaking on video from bullet points, is to print them out and tape them to a surface beside the camera—out of sight of the interviewer. Be sure to practice so you look natural. The secret is to grab a bullet point or group of points with your eyes, and when you have them in your mind, turn to your screen and deliver them while looking at your audience. This way, you won't appear to be reading.

#2 Design Your Set

Your setting will say a lot about you. If you have an in-person interview, you'll have little control over the stage that has been offered to you. But once you are in the conference room, try to take a chair that is at an angle to—not opposite—the interviewer. Sitting opposite can create a feeling of polarity. Sitting adjacent warms things up.

If your interview is virtual, create an appropriate background. I recently saw a clip of a leader speaking on Zoom. Behind him was a wooden bookcase crammed full of things that were so distracting I couldn't take my eyes off them. Among them were a college hoodie, a plant that needed watering, a cactus, a book on bulldogs with a bulldog staring at me from the cover of the book, a few empty vases, four or five books in disarray, and a sketch of an unknown building. I don't remember a thing the speaker said—I just remember these images. Imagine if he were being interviewed for a job. The interviewer would probably end up wondering, "When did you last water that plant?" or "Do you have a bulldog?" You don't want to create this visual distraction.

Think of the background as your stage.

Begin by choosing an area with good lighting. Avoid sitting in front of windows that can cast dark shadows or flood you with too much light.

Then, consider how professional your background looks. If you're interviewing from home, your backdrop should be businesslike—preferably a living room or study, not a bedroom or kitchen. If you're at work, an office or a conference room is great. Your background should be uncluttered and might include a bookcase, a vase of flowers, a lamp, a fireplace, or a photo of your family (but not all of these). Avoid virtual backgrounds with fake pictures of buildings or faraway places. Your interviewer will want to see you in your actual environment.

Make sure there is nothing that will move or make a sound: people coming in and out of the room, a dog barking, the noise of a printer, telephones ringing, delivery services, home repair people, or colleagues coming into your office or passing by your work station. Take time before the interview to set your stage so there will be no distractions.

Of course, you can't always control your setting. I know a young job candidate who was asked to take a phone call from a hiring executive on a Friday afternoon. She had made an appointment with a massage therapist just before the time of the interview, so she told me: "I planned to get out of the massage therapy session, go directly to a Starbucks nearby, and take the interview at a quiet table outside Starbucks. But as I sat outdoors, it was windy, and there was a big garbage truck that kept backing up next to me. I said to the VP interviewing me, 'I do apologize.'

But the good news was that he said, 'That's fine, I totally get it.'" And the job candidate realized that the boss was someone who was so accommodating she could really work for him. She got the job and loves it. Happy ending!

#3 Look the Part

What you wear to an interview makes a huge difference. JDP, an agency that specializes in background screening, makes this point in a recent study.[2] Research the way people dress in that company, and dress a cut above that. A job interview is a formal event, so for most interviews, choose clothes that you would wear if you were making a client presentation in that firm or having a meeting with senior management. That can mean wearing a suit or jacket, especially if you're being interviewed by a bank or a major institution. But if you're interviewing with a start-up or a creative agency, a well-pressed shirt or dress may be fine.

Make sure that your shoes are polished (if it's an in-person interview) and that your accessories are unobtrusive. A pair of dangling earrings, for example, can look out of place in a professional discussion and they can be a huge distraction in a video or virtual interview when so much of what you show is your upper body. If you're interviewing with a creative agency, you'll want stylish clothing and even an accent of jewelry. But make sure whatever you're wearing is not overly distracting.

#4 Unleash the Power of Your Script

Don't even think of going into an interview without a script to guide you. Your interview script will enable you to come across as clear, confident, and compelling. Without one, your off-the-cuff remarks will likely sound fragmented, and they'll not add up to a good story—or any story at all. Why risk it?

In chapter 13, we talked about five types of interview scripts.

Three of these are set pieces: the video (sent in advance), the presentation (delivered as an alternative to the typical back-and-forth discussion), and the demo (delivered at some point in the interview).

The two remaining interview scripts (the word-for-word and the bullet-point script) are more common. Even if you're pressed for time, it should be a no-brainer to create an interview script. Whether you've written out a verbatim script or created one in bullet point form, you'll want to get your points across as part of your dialogue. Once you develop the script, learn it and rehearse it. Do so until it is firmly in your mind as a structure that will guide you during the interview.

Here's how to use your script (designed with HIRE):

Deliver your hook as a greeting.

Early in the interview, inspire with your message.

As the discussion continues, convey the points in the reinforce part of your script.

At the end of your conversation, engage with your call to action.

This strategy will allow you to get your key messaging across—and enable you to feel you're not just a passive respondent but are communicating intentionally.

#5 Be Your Authentic Self

Being real, genuine, and open in an interview can make a huge difference between success and failure. You want to be someone people connect with. If not, you won't inspire their trust and you won't create that personal bond that interviewers look for.

Before the interview, think about how you want to come across. Ask yourself, "What qualities do I admire in myself?" "What do others respect in me?" "When did I really connect with someone I hadn't met before, and why was I able to?" See if you can draw from those questions answers that will enable you to project your best self. Review the characteristics in chapter 2, and decide which ones reflect your best qualities.

As well, go into the interview well rehearsed. Ironically, rehearsing your story—the lines in your HIRE script and answers to questions—will give you the confidence to be yourself. Think of it this way: you have to prepare to be spontaneous. The more you internalize what you want to say, the less you'll stumble over your lines or feel awkward. You'll have a good flow, purpose, and confidence. See chapter 5 for rehearsal techniques. All this preparation will help you deliver a genuine performance during the interview.

#6 Project a Strong Presence

Good body language is critical in job interviews. Nonverbal cues make up 60 to 80 percent of face-to-face communication. Although Zoom or video interviews may not allow you to communicate with body language as fully as live interactions do, what the interviewer does see will be scrutinized more closely. Here's how to project a strong presence:

- **Use strong eye contact.** Look directly at the interviewer. Don't look down or around; you'll appear less confident. Eye contact will make your message feel personal and direct. Research indicates that influential people tend to look longer at others than less dominant people do.[3] Be generous with your eye contact. In a group interview, make sure to give an equal amount of eye contact to each person, regardless of their rank.

- **Smile warmly and frequently.** You will be judged by your ability to connect with people, and a good smile does just that. But beware of a smile that's pasted on or constant.

Think of using an inner smile that reflects genuine enjoyment and empathy. It's the kind of smile that lights up your face and lights up the relationship.

- **Sit tall.** If you slouch, you're saying you're tired and not engaged. Sitting tall shows that you are fully present. It's not so much how tall we actually are that conveys stature; it's how tall we make ourselves by sitting up straight.

- **Position yourself to create rapport.** Sitting too far back in a Zoom call distances you and can create visual distractions for the interviewer. But sitting too close to your screen can make you look like a talking head. You'll want the gestures of your arms to show. The secret is to sit as far away from your laptop as you would sit from an interviewer in an in-person situation.

- **Gesture warmly.** Don't fold or cross your arms—you'll look defensive or closed. Avoid awkward "flipper" gestures created by elbows tucked into your body. Keep your arms open and gesture with the full arm in the direction of the interviewer. Avoid weak wrist gestures and keep your hands open; don't hold them, fold them, or flatten them on the table.

- **Be still when you're listening and often when you're talking.** Stillness is powerful. This does not mean being stiff. It means not having random movements like touching your face, fixing your hair, fidgeting, or restlessly moving in your chair. Such movements suggest you are not at ease with the interview—and they will only be exaggerated in a digital interview.

- **Speak with energy.** Accept that the stakes are high and that you want to bring energy to the interview.

High-energy people are more charismatic, they inspire others, and they are more likely to come across as focused and excited about the position. Moving into a heightened state of energy will transform any nervousness into positive energy and passion. You will show that you really care. If you have back-to-back virtual interviews, it's easy to get fatigued—Zoom is an energy buster! Find your own pre-talk ritual to pump yourself up, as presentation coach Nancy Duarte suggests,[4] and grab your energy whatever way you can.

- **Modulate your voice.** Doing so will enable you to indicate what's important, and what's less important. This will help your audience be less fatigued than if you were to deliver everything with equal emphasis.

- **Pause between your thoughts.** Most people don't pause enough—but pauses are important in interviews. A pause before answering a question makes you appear more thoughtful. And pausing between ideas will allow your interviewer to process what you've said.

- **Laugh.** Happiness is contagious. If you show that you are naturally a fun person who can bond with people, even virtually, you're more likely to build rapport with your interviewers and get that coveted job.

#7 Ask Great Questions

Asking questions and listening carefully to the answers will create warm ties with your interviewer and give you a better understanding of the company and how it would be to work for that enterprise.

A study by the Harvard University Social Cognitive and Affective Neuroscience Lab revealed that people don't reach out enough and let others talk. They spend 60 percent of their conversations talking about themselves, and when they're not talking about themselves, they are thinking about what to say next.[5] Don't be that person. Ask questions and listen carefully to show respect for the interviewer and indicate that you are fully invested in the job.

Noah Yashinsky, who landed a top sales position at Amazon, told me that it's "absolutely" necessary to ask questions in an interview: "Questions show you're invested in that company."

"What questions did you ask when you got that job?" I inquired.

He replied: "The first one I asked was about the interviewer. I researched my five Amazon interviewers on LinkedIn. One had come from Yahoo!, where he had worked for 10 years. I asked him about his responsibilities at Yahoo! and why he felt compelled to join Amazon. I asked similar questions to the other interviewers to show I was invested in them. My second question was about the job. I was applying for a sales job, so I'd ask: 'What does a prototypical sales person look like?'"[6]

The questions you ask can be about the company and its culture, the job and the team, or the manager who would be your boss.

Questions about the company and its culture might include the following:

1. How would you describe your company's overall purpose?

2. What do you like about working for this company?

3. Will I be able to work from home or work from anywhere?

4. What opportunities are there for advancement?

5. How would you describe the culture of the company?

6. What is the company's commitment to diversity and inclusion?

7. How would you describe your firm's leadership?

Questions about the job and the team you'd be working with show you are keen to work in that role. Tejal Wagadia, a career expert at Jobscan who has interviewed close to 10,000 individuals over the past seven years, encourages candidates to ask pointed questions about the job. "When you have no questions of this kind," she says, "you will appear not to be interested in the position."[7] Wagadia's favorite questions are:

1. What does success in this job look like in the first 90 days?

2. What problems are being solved by the team right now?

3. What is the #1 stakeholder complaint you have heard about the team?

4. What is it about my background that would add value to your current team?

5. How do you communicate when someone isn't meeting their monthly goals?

Finally, you might ask probing questions about your future boss and that individual's goals. Zanzibar Vermiglio, managing partner of Zanzibar Enterprises, suggests that "the number one thing job candidates can do to increase their chances of getting hired, is to ask really pointed questions about the issues, problems, and goals the hiring manager—and the candidate's potential future boss—has for the department."[8] These are Vermiglio's gutsy questions to ask the manager or future boss:

1. What are you really trying to make happen?
2. What are the things you're struggling with right now?
3. What's happening in the company at large?
4. How does your department interact with other departments?
5. Are there any problems in these relationships?
6. What did the last person in this job achieve?
7. What does your career look like next, and how will this role help you get there?

Whether you're asking about the company, the culture, the job, or the boss, the best questions come only after you've done your research. If you ask a banker "What products do you offer?" they'll wonder why you didn't read materials that were readily available.

The best time to ask questions is when the formal part of the interview is over. The hiring manager usually will say, "Do you have any questions?" By asking questions, you can open up the discussion and, in doing that, strengthen your connections with the interviewer. Questions also put the interview on a more personal footing. Asking questions means that the interview will be a true exchange—a dialogue rather than an inquisition.

To show you are engaged in listening, take notes. Bring pen and paper to the interview, and jot down things the interviewer says. This will impress the interviewer, who will see that you are serious about what she says. This is also important because, in the heat of the moment, you might forget precisely what was said. Taking good notes also means you can build on what you learn in one interview and take that insight into the next. A job candidate who went through seven interviews for a single job said she was told she got the job because she had shown she was able "to grow with the feedback along the way and translate it into the next interview. This shows us how you will grow into this role."

Chris Kowalewski, chief growth officer for Compass Group, sums up the power of listening when he says, "In evaluating job candidates, I ask, 'Do they ask good questions? Have they done their research? And do they take notes?' It should be a dialogue, a conversation."[9]

#8 Stay Strong

Being interviewed can cause jitters—so don't worry if you feel nervous. That's normal in such high-stakes situations. But don't let your tremors make you feel bad—bad about yourself or bad about the interview. Don't let yourself feel diminished or powerless. Stand your ground as someone who deserves to be heard.

According to research by Julie McCarthy, a professor of organizational behavior and HR management at the Rotman School of Management, "While job interviews have always been stressful, for many, the pandemic-related transition to remote interviews has exacerbated the problem." McCarthy says that "the change of format is less comfortable to those who haven't engaged in a remote interview before. Recorded interviews can add to anxiety, while the ability to see your own image on-screen has proven to be emotionally taxing."[10]

Intense preparation of the kind recommended in this book will go a long way to helping you deal with your nerves. High achievers I've spoken to say they take weeks to prepare—weeks devoted to crafting interview scripts, rehearsing them, preparing answers to questions, and mastering their lines. To build your confidence you might even have a mantra that you repeat to yourself as you go into the interview. It might be, "I know I'd be great in this role," or "I'm 100 percent prepared," or simply, "I've got this!"

But even with all this prep work, it can be tough to maintain your composure during interviews, particularly if you find you're not getting the feedback you crave. Some interviewers may seem indifferent; others can be aggressive and challenging.

When I applied for my first job, I was interviewed by a pull-no-punches senior executive who lashed away at me for over an hour. I was eight months pregnant and sweating in a wool dress. But I held my own, and for every question he hurled at me, every challenge he raised, I stood strong. When the interview was over, I rushed to a pay phone to call my husband and tell him: "This guy hated me." But that wasn't the case. He was testing me. He wanted to see if I had the mettle to work in an aggressive, high-tech organization. A few days later, I received a job offer from him, with a salary more than twice what I had expected—and I accepted.

He became my best-ever mentor. He taught me to hold my own in any situation. He said, "You're going to be writing speeches for executives who may be five levels above you. But you walk into their office and take charge." I was emboldened by those words, and I always held my own when I worked with an executive.

Hold your own in interviews, even if you're being interviewed by someone far more senior than you or who is in a position of power (able to hire you). And don't worry if someone interviewing you seems not to like you—you're not there to be liked. You're there to be *respected*. A tough interview allows you to earn respect, as long as you don't get freaked out by it.

In the same vein, don't be unsettled if the interviewer appears disengaged or distracted. That might have to do with something that happened to them that morning, or they may be taking calls because they have an urgent matter to resolve. It is not all about you, in other words. Even during your interview time, business continues. Hold your own by maintain a strong, confident attitude, rather than being thrown off by fears that you are not getting through.

Companies are looking for people with soft skills—individuals who are empathetic and comfortable with others. If you do all the things we've discussed in this chapter, you will show the character, confidence, and strength that win hiring managers over. As an added bonus, you will have a new set of skills that will serve you well in your entire career.

CHAPTER 19

Stay Connected, Stay in Touch

THE FINAL WORDS OF YOUR interviewer were "We'll be in touch." Yet days—and maybe even weeks—pass without any word. Your mind goes into a tailspin.

The position you applied for seemed like a perfect fit; you had a great interview, maybe several; you followed up with a thank-you note and then . . . nothing! That hurts because you feel like you've been ghosted. Over 75 percent of job seekers say they've been ghosted following an interview.[1] But a successful job seeker doesn't give up or let the ghost get the better of them. Stay focused, stay connected, and stay in touch.

And don't despair: there may be sound reasons for the delay. Many readers responded to a *Fast Company* article I wrote on ghosting by pointing out that despite their initial worries, the wait could be explained.[2] In one case, the executive who had done the interviewing had been let go. In another instance, a company-wide reorganization put everything on hold. In many cases, the candidates eventually heard from the company (and, in some instances, received very good news).

The Wrong Way to Follow Up

If you haven't heard back and you've given the company a reasonable amount of time to reply, it's important to follow up. There's a right way and a wrong way to reach out. Here's an example of what *not* to do in a follow-up email to the recruiter or hiring manager:

> Subject: Following Up on Assistant Manager, HR, Application
>
> Hi Derrick,
>
> I hope all is well. I know how busy you probably are, but I recently applied for the position of assistant manager, HR, and wanted to check in on your decision timeline. I am excited about the opportunity to join TriCo and help with your world-class programs. Please let me know if it would be helpful for me to provide any additional information as you move on to the next stage in the hiring process.
>
> I look forward to hearing from you,
> Leila Carillon

The language of this letter undermines the writer. The tone is, at times, too chummy, and at other times, too tentative. Starting off with "Hi" is overly casual. "Dear" is more professional. "I hope all is well" is also weak. It's not clear whether the job candidate is hoping the individual is well or that the job prospect is going well. In either case, this phrase suggests the possibility of an illness or a problem. The word "hope" creates a tentative tone.

Saying "I know how busy you probably are" is a no-no, because it implies that the hiring manager has more important things to do than to get back to the job candidate. "I wanted to check in" is weaker than saying "I am checking in." "Wanted" implies that something was desired but not done. The next sentence is quite good: "I am excited about" shows the candidate's excitement, though saying "help" weakens it. The last sentence begins with a weak request: "Please let me know if it would be helpful for me to provide any additional information." Suggesting that more information may be needed shows that the candidate is finding reasons why her interaction to date may have been insufficient.

It is understandable that a candidate who feels ghosted might write a letter that smacks of insecurity. But there is no reason to show that you might be feeling down. Retain a confident tone and keep your language strong.

The Right Way to Follow Up

The better way to follow up is to remain positive. Ask at the end of your interview when you can expect to hear from them and send a note of inquiry if you haven't heard back within that timeframe. If you still don't hear back, wait another week and then call, or find another channel for getting information. An assistant, for example, might explain to you the reasons for the delay.

When you do write that follow-up letter, keep your tone upbeat and your structure—guided by the HIRE template—clear. Continue to sell your candidacy (although not at the same length as in the cover letter you submitted with the resume or the thank-you note you sent after the interview).

Here is the previous letter, rewritten:

Subject: Following Up on Assistant Manager, HR, Application

Dear Derrick,

Hook
I am pleased to be a candidate for the assistant manager, HR, position and was delighted to meet with
you last month.

Inspire
Our conversation made me still more excited about this
opportunity, which would build upon my experience.

Reinforce
I have worked to create a diverse, empowered workforce,
like the one you are striving for. And I know I could
provide leadership for your world class HR programs.

Engage
Thank you for taking the time to meet with me, and
I'll await the interview with your vice president,
Ms. Angela Santelli.

Best regards,
Leila Carillon

As you can see, the revision is more confident and likely to receive a positive response. Use this guidance for any follow-up letter you write to anyone who has promised to be in touch and whose response is delayed. The bottom line: stay positive and use every opportunity to promote yourself as a strong candidate.

You've Landed the Job. Now What?

YOU'VE LANDED YOUR DREAM POSITION. Congratulations!

Celebrate your win! Thank everyone who helped you succeed. And as you embark upon your new role, realize you've acquired a powerful set of skills that will help you in the days ahead. The lessons in this book will serve you well in your new role and in your career. Your job search may be over—but the skills you've gained will contribute to your continuing success in the months and years to come. Here are the things to keep in mind.

Keep Telling Your Story

You are still the main character in this story you've been crafting—and it's far from over. This is your career story, and it will continue to be your story in this job and in the promotions and new dimensions that come your way. Don't stop thinking about what your career goals are, how you want to come across, what your message is, who your audience is, and what will make people want to work with you. All of this is part of your story.

Just as you took time to create the best narrative for the next stage in your career journey, you'll want to keep asking yourself, "Where do I want to go?" "What is my best opportunity as the next step in my career?" "What will make me feel I am using my talents?" "Do I want to work for a company, or work for myself?" And "what will make me feel I am doing my very best to bring value to the world by using my skills and experience?"

You literally will be "plotting" the story line of your career, as you ask yourself and answer these questions. I have had a long and meaningful career, and I can tell you from experience that I plotted every step of the way, from my first job to being entrepreneur of a successful company. I can tell you none of my decisions came easily; there was a lot of mental wrestling and, ultimately, decisions that moved me on to better terrain. Follow the steps outlined in this book to create a story for yourself that has an upward trajectory. And when you feel you've hit a wall, MOVE ON! Continue the journey, and make each step of the way more fulfilling, more worthy of your skills, and more centered on what you value.

Develop Your Character

In chapter 2, we looked at how you can project your best qualities in your job search. These same qualities will stand you well in your new role and in every role you assume throughout your career. So invest yourself in them.

#1 Be Authentic. There is no better quality to bring to work and share with your boss and colleagues than this one. In this new virtual and hybrid world of work, it's particularly important to share your genuine self—your ideas and values, your sense of humor, your stories, your successes, your challenges, your smiles, and, yes, your life outside of work. Let people get to know you—the real person behind the job title. If you do so, you will inspire their trust.

And by keeping yourself centered on your true qualities and feelings, you will be able to determine exactly what you want out of each job and out of your career as a whole.

#2 Be Positive. Your enthusiasm and positive energy helped you land your job. Demonstrate those same qualities in your current and future positions. Don't diss your last boss or your present one. Don't talk unfavorably about your colleagues. Speak enthusiastically about your job and your dedication to the role. Applaud the work of your team and your colleagues. Show that you believe in diversity and fair treatment for all. Carry this positive attitude with you every day in your new role and future jobs.

#3 Show Passion. Once you're in that new job, show the same passion for your work that you showed during your job journey. I saw a post on LinkedIn that impressed me because of the passion of this employee four months into her job. Her words: "It's been four months since my journey started with [my new company]. Never . . . ever . . . in my professional career have I experienced a better team culture. Never ever in my professional career have I experienced a C-level executive giving me a casual call in the afternoon. Never have I experienced professionalism with such dignity, inspiration, and grace. Never have I experienced a boss who laughs, let alone as much as me."

Such passion is contagious. If you demonstrate that enthusiasm, you will inspire your team and colleagues and you will stand out. And that passion will take you forward in your career to new roles and new opportunities. Make it your style.

#4 Convey Confidence. This sense of your value should shape your conversations and your language. To convey self-assurance, use verbs like "I know," "I believe," "we can," and "we will." Tackle projects with the same confidence you used to present your ideas to the interviewers. And show confidence in your people, your colleagues. Praise them.

This confidence will carry you forward in your career, to higher and higher levels of accomplishment. It will serve you well when you apply for jobs, and when you are in those roles. It will make others want to work for and with you, promote you, and champion you.

#5 Show Your Impact. Don't be afraid to showcase your accomplishments. Let people see the impact you are having—and be sure to do so in a way that is inclusive. No person does anything alone; show how your team, your mentor, your partners, and your colleagues played a role. And at every stage in your career, show that you have had an impact on others, on your company, on the world.

#6 Be Resilient. You needed that grit to stay upbeat during your search. Stay resilient as well in your job—times are uncertain, and life at work holds more ups and downs than it once did. Practice resilience and help others do so too. Don't let things get to you or those around you. Offer support if someone seems down. And be resilient in shaping your career—don't be afraid to let go of a role that no longer serves you; move on.

#7 Be Humble. It's the counterpart of confidence. A confident person doesn't have to boast. Stay humble, and others will respect you and want to be led by you.

#8 Be Respectful. This is another crucial quality to bring from your job search into work. Show a high regard for everyone regardless of their rank. Respect also means honoring deadlines and promises and realizing that everyone's time is valuable. Respect has grown ever more important as our workplaces become more inclusive. Respect others and you'll help set a tone for the office—and you will gain the respect of others. Respect will also allow you to honor those who hire you, advance you, and support you throughout your career journey.

#9 Show Gratitude. You've thanked everyone who helped you land that job. Now, show the same gratitude on the job and in subsequent roles. Every project involves a team effort. You succeed because of others. Be generous and thank everyone who assisted you. Every time someone impresses you, write them a handwritten note of thanks or give them a call to tell them they've done a great job. At the end of a meeting, tell your team you appreciate the opportunity to have them all present (even if it's a virtual call). Go out of your way to thank people—everyone needs these moments of recognition.

Prepare, Prepare, Prepare

You landed that job in part because you prepared intensively, each step of the way. In your new role and throughout your career, take this approach if you want to win over others.

Prepare for each meeting, each presentation to your colleagues or to executives, or for each pitch to clients as you did for the job interviews.

Preparation begins with research. Make sure to do your homework if you're meeting a client or a prospective customer. Study their company, their industry, their leadership, and their needs. Apply the same rigor to other encounters. Before meetings with colleagues or your boss, research what they're thinking about the project you'll be discussing. If you're meeting with a team, try to discover before the meeting where everybody stands.

Preparation includes mastering what you're going to say in any situation. On a Zoom call, an unprepared presenter might blurt out: "Let me see, I think there are some slides here," whereas a prepared presenter would say: "The next three slides will demonstrate the need we have for this product." Even if you're making an impromptu point at a meeting, pause before speaking to collect your thoughts so that you know exactly what you'll be sharing. Too many businesspeople rush to talk before they know what they want to say. The answer to selling yourself well is preparation.

Use HIRE: Your Superpower

The HIRE template helped you get the job. Continue to use it in every presentation and talk you give throughout your career.

Crafting scripts applies to everyday business situations as much as it did to the job search process. The elevator pitch is an important tool to carry with you whether you're in conversation with a colleague, a client, or a networking contact. You need to be persuasive in important meetings and client discussions. Make the HIRE scripting template a way of thinking, a mental process for acing your every meeting.

Suppose you're at a conference and you want to speak at next year's meeting. You approach the conference organizer and say:

Hook
It's great to meet you. This is an awesome
event. Congratulations on the success and the
large attendance.

Inspire
I'd love to speak at next year's conference—I've written extensively on the topic and believe I could have a big impact.

Reinforce

1. My most recent book is on empathetic leadership.

2. I know that's the theme of next year's conference.

3. And I would bring in some new research findings.

Engage
Let's set up a call to discuss.

Take another situation: imagine your boss calls you in and says "How is project X coming along? I've just found out management wants it completed sooner than I expected." Instead of twisting and turning and saying, "Uh, well, we've had a few meetings, not sure exactly how far along we are," come forward on the spot with a hook ("Glad you asked") and an inspiring message ("It's moving forward with good success"). Then reinforce ("We've accomplished three things—we've formed a team, set specific goals, and are well on our way to fulfilling them"). End by engaging ("I'll give you an update later today, and I am sure we can meet management's request"). When you internalize the template, these well-structured responses flow from your tongue easily.

HIRE delivers clear messaging. If you use it consistently, you will project clarity and confident leadership.[1] It will provide a powerful structure for all your communications throughout your career. It will ensure that you are always clear, message-based, and persuasive in your speaking and writing.

Nurture Your Network

You now know from your job search that networking works. Keep building your network.

Within your company, get to know your colleagues—not only those on your team, but individuals in other departments, as well as those above you and below you in the hierarchy. Building relationships across and up and down the organization means that you'll have a broader base of people who might hear of opportunities for you—within and beyond your company—when you're ready to move to the next role.

Getting to know those more senior than you is particularly important because these can be your high-level champions—people who can make a case for you when you're ready to move up the ladder. They may sponsor you when there is an opening in your firm, and they might mentor you if you ask. Should you choose to move outside your company, they will be there to endorse you by writing a note or making a call recommending you to someone in another company.

Networking outside your company should also be a way of life. Get to know the decision-makers in your industry by attending conferences, seminars, and networking events. Think about the kind of folks you'll need support from if you seek a job outside your company. Stay in touch with college friends, business school associates, professors, and anyone who might provide a referral when you're ready to look for that next job. And keep building your network through LinkedIn and other social media channels.

Stay Alert to Opportunities

You've come far by winning this one job—but it is only one of many that will represent your full career story. Think of it as a chapter in your larger narrative, with much ahead to be written. The next chapter might involve a new assignment in your present company or a new employer—or a career shift to something different.

Stay alert to all these possibilities.

If you're happy with the firm you are now with, explore opportunities that your employer is making available to you. Companies value loyalty and are increasingly determined to hold on to their talent, so they are posting jobs, offering upskilling and training opportunities, and providing career path education. Avail yourself of these opportunities and seek out jobs in your firm that build your capabilities. Should you decide to move on from your current employer, think about what you want when you are applying for that next position—and follow the steps we've discussed in this book.

Remember: you are writing the story. It's yours to create, chapter by chapter. Make it a compelling story, one that you'll be proud of every step of the way.

• • •

The Job Seeker's Script will enable you to tell your story successfully and land the job you desire. At the heart of a successful journey are scripts that enable you to persuade your listeners each step of the way. The HIRE template featured in this book will enable you to communicate convincingly and land that coveted role.

The skills you take away from reading this book will continue to bless you. This book provides the map for a journey that does not end with that next dream job. Every encounter and every interaction—whether you're looking for a new employer, advancing within a company, or pitching an important project—is part of the narrative you're creating for yourself and can share with the world. It's your unfolding story, and I am honored to be traveling this path with you.

Acknowledgments

THIS BOOK IS A COLLABORATION, and I thank everyone who generously contributed to it.

My appreciation begins with The Humphrey Group clients who, over a 30-year period, gave me their trust, shared their stories, worked with me to become inspiring speakers and leaders, and even invited me to coach their family members for upcoming college and job interviews. Many examples in this book, told anonymously, derive from my clients.

Another group I'm deeply indebted to are the senior executives who shared their ideas with me in interviews. Their insights have shaped this book. These executives include Emily He, corporate vice president, business applications marketing, Microsoft; Mike Hudy, chief science officer, Modern Hire; Chris Kowalewski, chief growth officer, Compass Group; Nagaraj Naudendla, senior vice president, product development, Oracle; Brett Tearney, vice president, HR service delivery management, ServiceNow; Mark Unak, chief technology officer, Forj, and former chief technology officer, Harqen; Zanzibar Vermiglio, managing partner, Zanzibar Enterprises; and Cynthia Ward, vice president, The Humphrey Group.

I also thank the recruiters, career counselors, and hiring managers I spoke with. This wonderfully helpful group includes Marissa Dyck, vice president, people and operations, The

Humphrey Group; Amanda Luthra, a senior freelance recruiter; Tejal Wagadia, career expert, Jobscan; Mikele Watters, head of Mikele Watters Coaching; and Jodyi Wren, interim assistant dean, executive director, and assistant vice provost, Career Education Initiatives, University of Rochester.

Many millennials generously shared their job search stories and showed how to get it right and succeed when going for your dream job. These inspiring young people include Alex Burstein, culture initiatives specialist, Calix; Ben Egnal, senior art director, Public Inc.; Teddy Moss, senior manager, Deloitte Digital; Michael Palombo, head of US content partner–led revenue, Twitter; Stacey Wollman, senior sales underwriter, The Hartford; Noah Yashinsky, senior account executive, Amazon US; and Fang Yu, strategist, Performance Art.

There are people in this book who are unnamed, and I have included their stories but quietly changed identifiers. I am indebted to them for sharing their narratives with me. My thanks as well to the individuals who read various drafts and shared their insights: Terry Dowling, Lilly Palmieri, Karen Milner, and Jared Lindzon. Their contribution made the book much richer.

I'd like to give a big shout-out to the *Fast Company* team—without whom this book would never have been written. I've been a contributor to this publication since 2015, and am grateful to *Fast Company* for giving me the opportunity to write for such an acclaimed publication. I also appreciate their encouraging me to incorporate material from these articles into this book. I thank my *Fast Company* editors—Kathleen Davis, Rich Bellis, and Julia Herbst—for being a dream team to work with. They have offered me valuable guidance over the years and let me write on topics that inspire me. I also thank Patrick Hainault, vice president of Mansueto Ventures, publisher of *Fast Company* and *Inc.*, who supported this book's publication and selected it for the prestigious Fast Company Press Imprint.

My appreciation also goes to Greenleaf Book Group, which transformed *The Job Seeker's Script* from a manuscript into an elegant, well-crafted book. This team has provided strong support to me every step of the way. Daniel Sandoval, my first contact at Greenleaf, waited patiently for the finished manuscript and applauded its arrival. Greenleaf's remarkable editorial, production, marketing, and distribution group has been professional and gracious. This team includes Erin Brown, Jared Dorsey, Danielle Green, Valerie Howard, Amanda Marquette, and Brian Welch (project manager). They are all experts in their own right, yet immensely supportive and collaborative. I highly recommend them as a publishing organization!

The final credits go to my family—with whom this story begins and ends. My husband, Marc Egnal, has always supported me and been a champion of every book I write. He has been a keen voice in my decision to author *The Job Seeker's Script*. Having written several books himself, he well knows the power of writing about what you love, and he knew I loved the idea of reaching out to job seekers and helping them through their journey. He is also a great editor and has read every word in this book.

My sons, Bart and Ben, strongly supported this project. Bart Egnal, my older son, took over The Humphrey Group in 2015, and as CEO of the firm, has continued to build that enterprise. Ben and his wife, Fang Yu, were also generous with their time and anecdotes, sharing their own job search experiences and introducing me to their friends whose stories are in this book.

Holden, our French bulldog who sleeps on the floor next to me as I write, deserves a mention, too. Without him, writing would have felt much lonelier.

Notes

INTRODUCTION

1. Adam Bryant, "Tobi Lütke of Shopify: Powering a Team With a 'Trust Battery'," *New York Times* Corner Office, April 22, 2016, https://www.nytimes.com/2016/04/24/business/tobi-lutke-of-shopify-powering-a-team-with-a-trust-battery.html.

CHAPTER 1: DECIDING ON YOUR STORY LINE

1. Lewis Carroll, *Alice's Adventures in Wonderland* (Macmillan, 1865).

2. "More than 80% open to new jobs: Accounting Principals and Ajilon," Staffing Industry Analysts, July 18, 2018, https://www2.staffingindustry.com/Editorial/Daily-News/More-than-80-open-to-new-jobs-Accounting-Principals-and-Ajilon-46765/.

3. Dinah Alobeid, "What every company needs to know about hiring right now: Key learnings from the 2022 Greenhouse Candidate Experience Report," Greenhouse, https://www.greenhouse.io/blog/key-learnings-from-the-2022-greenhouse-candidate-experience-report.

4. Jim Mandelaro, "College seniors hitting the job market should follow these tips," University of Rochester Newsletter, November 19, 2021, https://www.rochester.edu/newscenter/jobs-for-recent-college-graduates-tips-503062/.

5. Stephanie Vozza, "Welcome to the 'Great Resignation.' Should you quit your job too?" *Fast Company*, July 1, 2021, https://www.fastcompany.com/90651178/welcome-to-the-great-resignation-should-you-quit-your-job-too.

6. "Mission & Culture Survey 2019," Glassdoor, https://www.glassdoor.com/about-us/app/uploads/sites/2/2019/07/Mission-Culture-Survey-Supplement.pdf.

7. Amanda Stansell, "Which Workplace Factors Drive Employee Satisfaction Around the World?" Glassdoor Economic Research, July 11, 2019, https://www.glassdoor.com/research/employee-satisfaction-drivers/.

8. Universum, "Employer Branding NOW 2022," p. 12. Download this study at https://universumglobal.com/library/employer-branding-now-2022/.

9. Adam Grant, LinkedIn, https://www.linkedin.com/posts/adammgrant_before-taking-a-job-offer-its-worth-asking-activity-6636607274435567616-2BSY/.

10. Donald Sull and Charles Sull, "10 Things Your Corporate Culture Needs to Get Right," *MIT Sloan Management Review*, September 16, 2021, https://sloanreview.mit.edu/article/10-things-your-corporate-culture-needs-to-get-right/.

11. Kim Lyons, "Apple CEO Tim Cook tells employees the return to offices will begin on April 11," *The Verge*, March 4, 2022, https://www.theverge.com/2022/3/4/22961592/apple-april-11-return-office-corporate-pandemic-tim-cook. And Lucas Mearian, "Apple employees revolt against mandatory back-to-work policies," *Computerworld*, May 6, 2022, https://www.computerworld.com/article/3660071/apple-employees-revolt-against-mandatory-back-to-work-policy.html.

12. "The Born Digital Effect: Young Workers and the New Economy," Fieldwork by Citrix, 2021, https://www.citrix.com/content/dam/citrix/en_us/documents/analyst-report/work-2035-the-born-digital-effect.pdf.

13. Chris Kowalewski, interview by author, September 3, 2021.

CHAPTER 2: DEVELOPING YOUR CHARACTER

1. Liz Ryan, "12 Qualities Employers Look for When They're Hiring," *Forbes*, March 2, 2016, https://www.forbes.com/sites/lizryan/2016/03/02/12-qualities-employers-look-for-when-theyre-hiring/?sh=492053752c24.

2. Steven Greenberg, "Facebook's top recruiter: We want 'builders at heart,'" *CBS News*, March 16, 2018, https://www.cbsnews.com/news/facebooks-top-recruiter-we-want-builders-at-heart/.

3. Dipti Jain, "Hiring and retaining Gen Z talent," an interview with Akhil Saxena, LinkedIn News, January 17, 2022, https://www.linkedin.com/video/event/urn:li:ugcPost:6886202457928679424/.

4. Greenberg, "Facebook's top recruiter."

5. Judith Humphrey, "If you really want the job, show you have these 6 qualities," *Fast Company*, July 2, 2020,

https://www.fastcompany.com/90523307/
if-you-really-want-the-job-show-you-have-these-6-qualities.

6. Humphrey, "If you really want the job."

7. Greenberg, "Facebook's top recruiter."

8. Morgan Smith, "The 'No. 1 thing' all great resumes have in common, according to Google's head of recruiting," *CNBC Make It*, December 13, 2021, https://www.cnbc.com/2021/12/13/googles-head-of-recruiting -the-one-rule-to-writing-a-strong-resume-.html.

9. Stephanie Vozza, "How this tech company has achieved zero turnover since 2018," *Fast Company*, August 31, 2021, https://www.fastcompany.com/90669644/ how-this-tech-company-has-achieved-zero-turnover-since-2018.

10. Universum, "Employer Branding NOW 2022," p. 13. Download this study at https://universumglobal.com/library/ employer-branding-now-2022/.

11. Humphrey, "If you really want the job."

12. Smith, "The 'No. 1 thing.'"

13. Jared Lindzon, "Extreme ways CEOs are testing soft skills in job interviews," *Fast Company*, September 11, 2019, https://www .fastcompany.com/90399561/extreme-ways-ceos-are-testing -soft-skills-in-job-interviews.

14. Humphrey, "If you really want the job."

15. Giovanni Alesio, "Neuroscience: Link Between Gratitude and Happiness," *Profolus*, June 3, 2022, https://www.profolus.com/topics/ neuroscience-link-between-gratitude-and-happiness/.

CHAPTER 3: WHAT'S YOUR MESSAGE?

1. Amanda Luthra, interviews by author, June–September 2021.

CHAPTER 4: SCRIPT YOURSELF WITH HIRE

1. Emily Moore, "Stop Rambling! How to Tell a Concise, Compelling Career Story in an Interview," Glassdoor, August 9, 2018, https://www .glassdoor.com/blog/how-to-tell-a-career-story/.

CHAPTER 5: REHEARSE, REHEARSE, REHEARSE

1. Christy Ford, "How to answer common interview questions," Course Hero, https://www.coursehero.com/file/p2o2smp/The-first-thing-that-caught-my-eye-when-I-saw-the-position-posted-was-definitely/.

2. Michael Palombo, interview by author, October 29, 2021.

3. Noah Yashinsky, interview by author, December 1, 2021.

4. Palombo interview.

5. Yashinsky interview.

6. Adam Grant speech, American Express Business Class LIVE conference, July 20, 2022.

CHAPTER 7: NAILING THE NETWORKING CONVERSATION

1. Gina Belli, "How Many Jobs Are Found Through Networking, Really?" Payscale, April 6, 2017, https://www.payscale.com/career-advice/many-jobs-found-networking/.

2. Zameena Mejia, "How a cold call helped a young Steve Jobs score his first internship at Hewlett-Packard," Yahoo! Finance, July 26, 2018, https://finance.yahoo.com/news/cold-call-helped-young-steve-123000743.html.

3. Tejal Wagadia, interview by author, April 22, 2021.

4. Jim Mandelaro, "College seniors hitting the job market should follow these tips," University of Rochester Newsletter, November 19, 2021, https://www.rochester.edu/newscenter/jobs-for-recent-college-graduates-tips-503062/.

5. Steve Johnson, "I've always loathed networking. Here's why a virtual format makes it bearable," *Fast Company*, April 1, 2021, https://www.fastcompany.com/90621045/ive-always-loathed-networking-heres-why-a-virtual-format-makes-it-bearable.

6. Tejal Wagadia interview.

7. Gary Burnison, *Lose the Resume, Land the Job* (John Wiley & Sons: Hoboken, New Jersey, 2018), p.151.

8. "Three Weeks to Prepare a Good Impromptu Speech," http://quoteinvestigator.com/2010/06/09/twain-speech.

CHAPTER 8: PITCHING YOURSELF INSIDE YOUR COMPANY

1. Amy Adkins, "Millennials: The Job-Hopping Generation," *Business Journal*, Gallup, https://www.gallup.com/workplace/231587/millennials -job-hopping-generation.aspx.

2. "Career mobility outlook," Randstad RiseSmart Report, https://info .randstadrisesmart.com/career-mobility-outlook-report.

3. Universum, "Employer Branding NOW 2022," p. 4. Download this study at https://universumglobal.com/library/ employer-branding-now-2022/.

4. Emily He, email to author, January 15, 2021.

5. Stacey Wollman, interview by author, June 20, 2022.

6. Stacey Wollman interview.

7. Chris Kowalewski, interview by author, September 3, 2021.

CHAPTER 9: A WINNING RESUME

1. *The Future of Work 2022 Global Report*, https://media.monster.com/ marketing/2022/The-Future-of-Work-2022-Global-Report.pdf.

2. Michael Tomaszewski, "How to Write a Resume According to Science: A 2022 Study," ResumeLab, November 8, 2022, https://resumelab.com/ resume/how-to.

3. Tomaszewski, "How to Write a Resume."

4. "Why only 2% of applicants actually get interviews," Workopolis, November 10, 2016, https://careers.workopolis.com/advice/only-2-of -applicants-actually-get-interviews-heres-how-to-be-one-of-them.

5. Tomaszewski, "How to Write a Resume."

6. Nagaraj Nadendla, interview by author, March 19, 2021.

7. Kerri Anne Renzulli, "75 percent of resumes are never read by humans—here's how to make sure yours does," Yahoo! Finance, February 28, 2019, https://finance.yahoo.com/news/75-resumes-never -read-human-174855340.html.

8. Chris Rodgers, interview by author, July 7, 2020.

9. Paige Liwanag, "Don't Make These ATS Formatting Mistakes," Jobscan, February 25, 2021, https://www.jobscan.co/blog/ ats-formatting-mistakes/.

10. Nagaraj Nadendla, interview by author, March 19, 2021.

11. Brett Tearney, interview by author, June 15, 2021.

CHAPTER 10: A KILLER COVER LETTER

1. Michael Tomaszewski, "Is a Cover Letter Necessary in 2022? Do I Need a Cover Letter?" ResumeLab, August 10, 2022, https://resumelab .com/cover-letter/are-cover-letters-necessary.

2. Amanda Augustine, "Ask Amanda: Do I Really Need a Cover Letter?" TopResume, https://ca.topresume.com/career-advice/ is-a-cover-letter-necessary.

3. Peter Yang, "Cover Letters: Just How Important Are They?" ResumeGo, https://resumego.net/research/cover-letters/.

4. Regina Borsellino, "Finally, An Answer To: Are Cover Letters Still Necessary," The Muse, December 15, 2020, https://www.themuse.com/ advice/do-i-need-cover-letter.

5. Tomaszewski, "Is a Cover Letter Necessary."

6. Yang, "Cover Letters."

CHAPTER 11: HOW TO SAY THANK YOU

1. Chris Kowalewski, interview by author, September 3, 2021.

2. Andrew Seaman, "Thanks or no thanks? Should you send a thank-you note after a job interview?" LinkedIn News, July 26, 2021, https://www .linkedin.com/pulse/thank-thanks-should-you-send-thank-you-note -after-job-andrew-seaman/.

CHAPTER 12: ROCK YOUR RESEARCH

1. Chris Kowalewski, interview by author, September 3, 2022.

2. Interview with Jamie Dimon, Stanford Graduate School of Business, November 9, 2017, https://www.youtube.com/ watch?v=IyEadGANbgM.

3. Rich Cimini, "What happens in NFL head-coaching interviews? 'It's not about the X's and O's, it's about the CEOs,'" *ESPN*, January 6, 2022, https://www.espn.com/nfl/story/_/id/32994019/ what-happens-nfl-head-coaching-interviews-not-x-os-ceos.

4. "How the Great Resignation will shape HR and the Future of Work," Workhuman, https://www.workhuman.com/resources/research-reports/ how-the-great-resignation-will-shape-hr-and-the-future-of-work.

5. The Muse, https://www.themuse.com/companies.

6. "Shifting Tides: Changing Attitudes about Mental Health Care and

the Workplace," Modern Health, 2021, https://join.modernhealth.com/future-of-mental-health-2021-report-forrester.html.

7. Alyson Watson, "The one perk leaders need to be giving their burned out teams," *Fast Company*, October 22, 2021, https://www.fastcompany.com/90688840/the-one-perk-leaders-need-to-be-giving-their-burned-out-teams.

8. Stav Ziv, "How to Tell If a Company Actually Cares About Diversity and Inclusion, According to Ellen Pao," The Muse, https://www.themuse.com/advice/how-to-tell-company-cares-diversity-and-inclusion-ellen-pao.

9. Alex Burstein, interview by author, December 1, 2021.

10. Mike Hudy, interview by author, March 5, 2020.

11. Chris Kowalewski, interview by author, September 3, 2021.

12. Teddy Nykiel, "The 30-60-90 Day Plan: Your Secret Weapon for New Job Success (Template Included!)," The Muse, https://www.themuse.com/advice/30-60-90-day-plan-instructions-template-example.

13. Michael Palombo, interview by author, October 29, 2021.

CHAPTER 13: CRAFTING AN INTERVIEW SCRIPT

1. Michael Palombo, interview by author, October 29, 2021.

2. Noah Yashinsky, interview by author, December 1, 2021.

3. Alex Burstein, interview by author, December 1, 2021.

CHAPTER 14: PREPARING FOR Q&A

1. Tejal Wagadia, interview by author, April 22, 2021.

2. "Hiring insights from EY, finding a new role mid-career, and more job seeker news," LinkedIn's Get Hired Canada, December 20, 2021, https://www.linkedin.com/pulse/hiring-insights-from-ey-finding-new-role-mid-career-more-riva-gold/.

CHAPTER 15: MASTERING THE MOST COMMON QUESTIONS

1. Mikele Watters, interview by author, August 23, 2021.

2. Andrew Fennell, "How to update your resume so it shows what you learned during the pandemic," *Fast Company*,

August 10, 2021, https://www.fastcompany.com/90664171/
how-to-include-personal-development-skills-on-your-resume.

3. Claire Zillman and Emma Hinchliffe, "Incoming Citi CEO
    Jane Fraser says she's proof that working part-time isn't a career
    killer," *Fortune*, October 1, 2020, https://fortune.com/2020/10/01/
    citi-ceo-jane-fraser-career-advice/.

CHAPTER 16: BEING QUICK WITH QUIRKY QUESTIONS

1. Amanda Augustine, "Jobseekers: These 4 job interview responses are BS
    that hiring managers see right through," *Fast Company*, August 19, 2021,
    https://www.fastcompany.com/90666991/jobseekers-these-4-interview
    -responses-are-bs-that-hiring-managers-see-right-through.

2. Rich Cimini, "What happens in NFL head-coaching interviews?
    'It's not about the X's and O's, it's about the CEOs,'" *ESPN*,
    January 6, 2022, https://www.espn.com/nfl/story/_/id/32994019/
    what-happens-nfl-head-coaching-interviews-not-x-os-ceos.

3. Adam Bryant, "Neil Blumenthal of Warby Parker on a Culture of
    Communication," *New York Times* Corner Office, October 24, 2013,
    https://www.nytimes.com/2013/10/25/business/neil-blumenthal-of
    -warby-parker-on-a-culture-of-communication.html.

4. Lisa Eadicicco, "The trickiest questions Apple will ask in a job
    interview," *Business Insider*, April 10, 2015, https://www.businessinsider
    .com/trickiest-apple-interview-questions-2015-4.

5. Dominic Umbro, "21 tough interview questions you may have to
    answer if you want to work at Amazon," *Business Insider*, February 1,
    2018, https://www.businessinsider.in/21-tough-interview-questions
    -you-may-have-to-answer-if-you-want-to-work-at-amazon/
    articleshow/62746574.cms.

6. "15 Off-the-Wall Interview Questions You Should Know How to
    Answer," Forbes Coaches Council, November 6, 2018, https://www
    .forbes.com/sites/forbescoachescouncil/2018/11/06/15-off-the
    -wall-interview-questions-you-should-know-how-to-answer/
    ?sh=eeb112078d54.

7. "15 Off-the-Wall Interview Questions."

8. Tom Gerencer, "Illegal Interview Questions an Employer
    Cannot Ask," Zety, October 24, 2022, https://zety.com/blog/
    illegal-interview-questions.

9. William Poundstone, *How Do You Fight a Horse-Sized Duck?*: *Secrets to*

Succeeding at Interview Mind Games and Getting the Job You Want (Little, Brown Spark: New York, 2021).

10. William Poundstone, *Are You Smart Enough to Work at Google?: Trick Questions, Zen-Like Riddles, Insanely Difficult Puzzles, and Other Devious Interviewing Techniques You Need to Know to Get a Job Anywhere in the New Economy* (Little, Brown Spark: New York, 2012)

11. William Poundstone, *How Would You Move Mount Fuji?: Microsoft's Cult of the Puzzle—How the World's Smartest Companies Select the Most Creative Thinkers* (Little, Brown and Company: New York, 2004)

CHAPTER 17: TOP TALK: WHAT CEOS LOOK FOR

1. Ruth Umoh, "GM CEO Mary Barra has 3 favorite job interview questions and they all have the same answer," *CNBC*, https://www.cnbc .com/2018/12/17/gm-ceo-mary-barra-how-to-answer-her-favorite -interview-questions.html.

2. Umoh, "GM CEO Mary Barra."

3. Umoh, "GM CEO Mary Barra."

4. William von Hippel, Richard Ronay, Ernest Baker, Kathleen Kjelsaas, and Sean C. Murphy, "Quick Thinkers Are Smooth Talkers," *Psychological Science*, November 30, 2015, https://www .psychologicalscience.org/news/releases/quick-thinkers-are-charismatic .html.

5. Tim Cook, Q&A in Utah Tech Tour, October 1, 2016, https://www .youtube.com/watch?v=ZkV78RZ73Mw.

6. Leander Kahney, "How Steve Jobs finally persuaded a 37-year-old Tim Cook to join a near bankrupt Apple in 1998," *CNBC*, April 16, 2019, https://www.cnbc.com/2019/04/16/how-steve-jobs-persuaded -tim-cook-to-join-a-near-bankrupt-apple-in-1998.html.

7. Cook, Q&A in Utah Tech Tour.

8. Jamie Dimon, Stanford Graduate School of Business, November 9, 2017, https://youtu.be/IyEadGANbgM.

9. Indra Nooyi, *My Life in Full: Work, Family, and Our Future* (Portfolio/ Penguin: New York, 2021), p 141.

10. Morning Brew, Interview with Norah Ali, March 27, 2022, https:// www.youtube.com/watch?v=M_0fmnfQXI8.

11. Kimberly Weisul, "Spanx Founder Sara Blakely on How to Hire Senior Executives," *Inc.*, June 2015, https://www.inc.com/magazine/201506/ kimberly-weisul/sara-blakely-on-hiring-senior-executives.html.

CHAPTER 18: DELIVERING A STANDOUT PERFORMANCE

1. Patti Sanchez, *Presenting Virtually: Communicate and Connect with Online Audiences* (Duarte Press LLC, 2021), p. 15.

2. "The Experience of Interviewing in 2020," JDP, https://www.jdp.com/blog/the-experience-of-interviewing-in-2020/.

3. Sue Shellenbarger, "Is the boss looking at you? You'd better hope so," *The Wall Street Journal,* May 29, 2013, https://www.wsj.com/articles/BL-ATWORKB-962.

4. Nancy Duarte, "How to Pump Yourself Up Before a Presentation (or Calm Yourself Down)," *Harvard Business Review,* July 18, 2018, https://hbr.org/2018/07/how-to-pump-yourself-up-before-a-presentation-or-calm-yourself-down.

5. Adrian F. Ward, "The Neuroscience of Everybody's Favorite Topic," *Scientific American,* July 16, 2013, https://www.scientificamerican.com/article/the-neuroscience-of-everybody-favorite-topic-themselves/.

6. Noah Yashinsky, interview by author, December 1, 2021.

7. Tejal Wagadia, interview by author, April 22, 2021.

8. Zanzibar Vermiglio, interview by author, March 14, 2022.

9. Chris Kowalewski, interview by author, September 3, 2021.

10. Julie McCarthy, "Why businesses should strive for a more relaxing interview process," *Rotman Insights Hub,* March 2022, https://www-2.rotman.utoronto.ca/insightshub/talent-management-inclusion/job_interview_stress.

CHAPTER 19: STAY CONNECTED, STAY IN TOUCH

1. "What every company needs to know about hiring right now: Key learnings from the 2022 Greenhouse Candidate Experience Report," Greenhouse, https://www.greenhouse.io/blog/key-learnings-from-the-2022-greenhouse-candidate-experience-report.

2. Judith Humphrey, "4 things to do if you've been ghosted at work," *Fast Company,* February 9, 2022, https://www.fastcompany.com/90719441/4-things-to-do-if-youve-been-ghosted-at-work.

CONCLUSION: YOU'VE LANDED THE JOB. NOW WHAT?

1. The author's HIRE scripting template appears in her other books as "The Leader's Script," and it is a mainstay for those who aspire to lead.

About the Author

JUDITH HUMPHREY is a communications expert and the founder and former CEO of The Humphrey Group. This company teaches clients all over the world how to communicate successfully in high-stakes interviews, media events, presentations, and Q&A. She has built her career around coaching professionals at all levels on how to create clear and compelling narratives.

In addition to *The Job Seeker's Script*, Judith has authored three books: *Speaking as a Leader: How to Lead Every Time You Speak* (2012); *Taking the Stage: How Women Can Speak Up, Stand Out, and Succeed* (2014), and *Impromptu: Leading in the Moment* (2017). She also is a regular contributor to *Fast Company*; many chapters in this book, in fact, began as articles in that publication.

Judith strongly believes that if you script yourself clearly and learn your lines well, you will come across authentically and land your dream job. She knows this from the many job seekers, at all levels, she has successfully coached. When Judith is not writing books or coaching job candidates, she can be found playing her 100-year-old violin or hanging out with her French bulldog. Born, raised, and educated in the US, she lives in Toronto with her husband, Marc Egnal. They have two sons.

You can find Judith at www.judithhumphrey.com